THE JOURNEY IS HOME

John Sam Jones realised he was gay as a teenager at the beginning of the 1970s and quickly came to understand that his life would be lived always on the edge.

His collection of short stories – *Welsh Boys Too* – was an Honor Book winner in the American Library Association Stonewall Book Awards. His second collection, *Fishboys of Vernazza*, was short-listed for the Wales Book of the Year, which was followed by the novels *With Angels and Furies* & *Crawling Through Thorns*.

In 2001 he became the first co-chair of the LGB Forum Cymru (which was later renamed Stonewall Cymru), set up to advise the Welsh Government on LGB issues.

After working in ministry, education and public health for more than thirty years, John Sam Jones lives in semi-retirement with his husband in a small German village a stone's throw from the Dutch border.

THE
JOURNEY
IS HOME

Notes from a life on the edge

John Sam Jones

PARTHIAN

Parthian, Cardigan SA43 1ED
www.parthianbooks.com
© John Sam Jones 2021
ISBN print: 978-1-914595-10-3
ISBN ebook: 978-1-912681-95-2
Editor: Richard Davies
Cover Design: Marc Jennings
Printed by 4Edge Limited
Published with the financial support of the Books Council of Wales
British Library Cataloguing in Publication Data
A cataloguing record for this book is available from the British
Library.

"Not everything that is faced can be changed,
but nothing can be changed until it is faced."
– James Baldwin

Contents

I

Until one day in June

Before meeting Jupp I'd lived for three years in California, so the idea of living abroad didn't deter me from falling in love with him. We discussed the possibility of moving to his *Heimat*, more in the early years, but he'd always wind up those conversations with, 'I'm comfortable here... I've always felt welcome here... I'm happy here with you... there's no reason to move away – and besides, the bloated German bureaucracy stifles everyday life and the bloated middle-aged men wear pastel colours that look ridiculous... even the gay ones, who you'd think would know better.' Thirty years, then – a decade each in Liverpool, the Wirral and Ardudwy on the northwest coast of Wales.

Until one day in June.

Over those three decades our lives, our families, our friends, our cultures and our languages – they've all got mixed up. His accented English is shot through with German and the odd Welsh sweet-nothing. We speak English together but I swear at him in Welsh, which always makes him laugh, taking the sting from my scorn, and sometimes I'll echo one of his turns of phrase... we'll often eat 'rests' instead of left-overs and when he's grumpy I'll say, 'What's made you so *quengelisch*?' He's learned to pronounce my family's difficult names; to his eye some had no vowels! I've learned the German names of his kinfolk... and just a few phrases to get by... but languages, and grammar especially, have never been a talent I could boast about. When I'm sad, or sick, or worried, he cares for me. When he's upset or unsettled, when he's anxious about his work at the university or his ageing parents, or when he was grieving the death of his younger brother, I'd 'fuss'. That's how it's been in our long life together... it's what love does.

My family has lived in Barmouth, pressed between the Rhinog Mountains and Cardigan Bay, for three hundred years. In recent times tourists have discovered our beaches and castles, our hiking country and ancient standing stones, and tourism has become the life blood of the local economy. For more than a century, before the ubiquity of the family car, the railway link brought generations of west Midlands working folk to the mid-Wales coastal towns and villages for their summer holidays and family traditions of a week or a fortnight at the seaside became established. By 1962, a British Railways (Western Region) poster advertised Barmouth on station platforms throughout the United Kingdom as the *Queen of the Cambrian Coast*... by this time, too, many a farmstead and Victorian hovel had been vacated by locals – either moving away for work or moving into the newly built council houses (with running water, electricity and an inside toilet) – and second homes were being bought up by newly affluent city dwellers. Many an English in-comer, finding the old Welsh names too difficult, and with little regard for either the Welsh language or culture, dotted the Welsh landscape with English: 'Sea View' and 'Driftwood Cottage', 'Ridge Crest' and 'Panorama Lodge'.

Of course, deep friendships were forged between the Welsh and the English, and local boys and girls 'married out' after holiday romances blossomed – mixing genes, sharing traditions and weaving new histories. But often, too, there were misunderstandings that festered for decades – especially when the monoglot Union flag-wavers complained that the locals only spoke Welsh to spite them and exclude them from conversation... and so developed a tendency to blame 'the Brummies' for all the litter on the beach, for the dog fouling along the promenade, for the drunken brawls and vomit splattered pavements – and there was often relief when they drove their cars back over Offa's Dyke. Some in-comers have settled; few have bothered to learn the old language, but you'll still hear Welsh spoken over the garden walls and on the quay side despite Barmouth's reputation as 'far-west-Birmingham'. In the cliff-top graveyard I can point out the weavers and blacksmiths, the carpenters and bakers... the great, the great-great and the great-great-great grandparents.

My husband is from a village on the edge, where the Dutch border cuts across the field behind the last row of houses' back gardens. In the winter, the old border post, its engraved number crusted with lichen, leans awkwardly towards the Netherlands, an occasional perch for buzzards in the flat, grey landscape; in high summer the post is stranded in a golden shimmer of barley, or sometimes lost when the maize grows tall. The village was ravaged in the closing weeks of the war, first, by the Nazis seeking to defend their border, then by the allies seeking to oust the Nazis, and finally – meticulously – by the Dutch from the village on the other side who'd suffered unspeakable hardship during the occupation; they looted, believing that whatever they could carry was their due. The family homes that Jupp's parents built – one fairly modest house at the beginning of the sixties, the other, larger and 'architect designed' in 1972 (reward from the lucrative contracts with the British military his father had won to service the heating, plumbing and electrics on their nearby bases) give no clue to Ernst-Peter and Jutta's peasant origins. For centuries, Jupp's people had worked the local baron's land, cut wood from the forest that surrounded them to burn in their stoves, poached the baron's hares – no one dared take one of his deer or wild boar – and scratched out a life that bent their backs and made them old before they were forty.

Our early life together, with a double income and no

kids, had been more than comfortable. Even after my semi-retirement on health grounds at the age of fifty-five we were never going to starve: our house was paid-off, our home perhaps a bit too much like something out of one of those glossy magazines. Our B&B guests loved the hardwood floors and Persian carpets, the hand-made furniture from Welsh oak, the clutch of cherished original paintings, the fresh flowers on the dining table... and good wines and a choice of malt whiskies to lubricate those discussions late into the night after an evening meal or a weekend dinner party. We flew regularly around Europe, sometimes just to see friends for a night or two, or to lie for a week on a sunny beach to break the northern winter gloom; perhaps to explore a city we'd read about in one of the Saturday travel supplements... or even to catch an opera at La Fenice or the Liceu that, for some reason, hadn't been staged in Britain. And there were books, many hundreds of them.

Of course, David Cameron hadn't conceived that his Tory party, with its Euro-sceptics, would win a majority in the 2015 General Election. Confounding the opinion polls, they won a working majority and one of his first tasks as the new Prime Minister was to set in motion the legislation required to hold the promised referendum on membership of the European Union despite there being no considered vision for a Britain outside the EU.

It was clear to us that our lives benefitted from EU membership. We found it difficult to discuss pros and cons because Britain's relationship with its EU partners obviously entailed details that we couldn't begin to guess at, but which, nevertheless, touched our lives each day – safety standards of all kinds, workplace protections, food hygiene regulations, scientific and medical research, pharmaceuticals, rights to fly over one another's territories... and what about all the EU nationals who worked in the NHS and all the multi-nationals who employed tens of thousands, if not hundreds of thousands in the UK? And didn't we benefit directly from the peace in Northern Ireland? The IRA had often bombed targets on our side of the Irish Sea. Might a hard EU border jeopardise the Good Friday Agreement?

As an international couple who flew frequently around Europe we took 'free movement of people' for granted and couldn't begin to understand what negative impact may ensue if Britain withdrew from such an agreement. Were we destined to stand in different queues at immigration and passport control? Would my husband's residency after thirty years in the UK be questioned or made more difficult?

The Brexit debate gathered momentum. On both sides, half-truths and untruths were trotted out... both sides, unfortunately, managing to mislead and denigrate democracy. Husbands and wives disagreed; brothers and sisters argued; neighbours fell out; youngsters rolled their eyes at older people's insularity. Immigration, due to the free movement of people within the EU, became a primary issue for many; the relatively insignificant things that are different between people becoming divisive. Many people lost sight of the reality that we share so much more in common than any particular characteristic that separates us. The 'immigrants' were taking our jobs... 'they' were claiming our generous social security benefits and sending the money home... 'they' were changing the nature of our society so that you were as likely to hear Polish spoken in the street as you were English; for many in Wales the irony screamed – for hadn't England and the English sought to stamp out the Welsh language and ignore our culture for generations? It was as if the Brexit debate had granted license in some to express a latent xenophobia and a long-suppressed racism. The call to 'take back the control' supposedly relinquished to 'that unelected lot in Brussels' became a battle cry.

"I don't like the atmosphere this is creating," I said over supper one day.

"I'm starting to feel uncomfortable here," Jupp said. "I'm one of these 'immigrants' they're talking about."

In the days before the referendum, standing in the supermarket check-out line – in my trolley some cheeses from France and Holland, wine and oranges from Spain, olive oil from Italy, olives from Greece, blueberries from

Poland, and chocolate from Belgium – a conversation was struck up.

"I'm voting to leave," said the woman in front of me to the man before her.

"Me too," he said. "Too many bloody immigrants here now."

The woman at the cash register – Branca according to her name badge – shifted in her seat. Sensing her discomfort I said,

"My husband is German so let's just think twice before we talk about *bloody immigrants*."

Branca smiled at me;

"I'm from Portugal," she said, "but my kids were born here and they speak Welsh."

"Oh, we don't mean you, Branca," the woman who'd started it all said.

"So who do you mean?" I asked.

"Well... the blacks and the Poles," she said with a swagger.

"My cardiologist is a Welsh-speaking black woman from Cardiff... and without her I'd probably be dead," I said, "...and do you not know that hundreds of Polish pilots helped the RAF win the Battle of Britain?"

Into the awkward silence my words had beckoned, the man at the front, now packing his shopping, said, "Well, we need to take back control from those unelected bureaucrats in Brussels."

"Sounds to me as if you've never voted in the European parliament elections," I said.

Fuck you, you queer bastard, he mouthed as he lifted his bags from the counter.

We were drinking gin and tonic before supper and I couldn't decide whether I wanted to tell Jupp about the incident in the supermarket. Being called queer was something I'd learnt to shrug off after almost half a century of such name-calling, but I was unsettled by how free those two in the queue had felt to be so openly nasty. As an isolated incident it perhaps wouldn't have taken on such significance, but every day in *The Guardian* there were reports of a rise in xenophobic, racist and homophobic incidents in the weeks since the Brexiteers had begun to whip up emotions about difference – and putting the 'great' back into Britain. I hadn't thought through my response, so I took a different tack.

"I don't want to lose my European citizenship," I said. "How long would I have to live in Germany before I could become a citizen?"

"Because we're married I think it would be fairly automatic after three or four years," he said. "But it won't come to that..."

"But what if...?"

He made a long sigh, puffing out his cheeks and said, "If Britain leaves the EU you probably wouldn't be able to have joint citizenship; Germany only grants that to other EU members... and to the Turks because of that whole *Gastarbeiter* history."

"And I suppose I'd have to be able to speak German?"

"I wouldn't worry too much about that. In three or four years, if you lived there, even with your 'gift' for languages and that 'block' you have about grammar... you'd just pick it up," he said. "But how would you feel about giving up your British citizenship?"

It was my turn to sigh.

"You know that I've always thought of myself as Welsh first... so my British passport, my current 'legal status' as a British citizen, doesn't really say anything about who I understand myself to be... so I'd still be just as Welsh if all the legal paperwork was German."

"I really can't see it coming to that," he said, with a reassuring smile.

He took a long slug of his gin. "And I'm not sure I'd choose to settle in Germany... God, all those men in lime green three-quarter shorts and baby-blue tee shirts." He shook his head. "And all that formality... when I worked at the university all of the Germans involved in the triple diploma used to *Sie* one another – it was always *Herr Doktor* this and *Frau* that – as if we didn't have first names. Maybe we could go to Portugal or Spain?"

Our house went up for sale less than a week after the Brexiteers celebrated their victory in the referendum... so deep was our disappointment, so bitter our sense of having been betrayed. We calculated, with retirement lump-sums, pensions, savings and what we hoped to get for the house, that we could live – all be it frugally – for thirty years... and if either of us were to reach ninety we'd have to find a rich young man to care for us! The estate agent valued the house at a lower price than we'd hoped, despite our protestations about the location, the views over the estuary to Cadair Idris, the renovations and the lucrative B&B turn-over... but we pitched it higher believing we could always drop the price if we needed to.

We flew to Majorca for a few days – to scout – and realized that Palma and the communities close-by were too expensive; in-comers, mostly Germans, had forced the prices up, just like the English had forced up the prices in the scenic parts of rural Wales. Back home, a couple from the West Midlands came to view the house; they seemed interested.

After a long weekend with friends in Barcelona we concluded that the smell from the drains in the summer heat made for an unappealing prospect but that Vilanova, close to Sitges was very doable.

We agreed to sell to 'cash buyers' from Stratford who wanted a holiday home. They offered the asking price without a quibble and we swallowed our reservations about selling to English second-homers. Our next-door neighbour for four years, Barmouth's *Plaid Cymru* County Councillor, had sold to an English family the year before and somehow this made it alright for us to do the same... but, on reflection, that's such a feeble justification. Neither of us liked the couple buying our house, but it would be a quick sale and we took it as a sign that fate was with us and that turning our backs on Brexit Britain was the right thing to do.

A short trip to the eastern Algarve, to Tavira, where we'd been on holiday many years before, didn't live up to our memories and we realised that the influx of tourists in the summer months would make for uncomfortable living.

The exchange and completion dates on our house were set – it had taken nine months from that day in June. And during these months Jupp's younger brother died.

Gerd's death was very sudden. The headaches had lasted only a few days, but they were severe and wouldn't abate. His family doctor sent him for a scan to the local hospital. There was something there... so he was transferred to the university hospital in Aachen where they diagnosed a tumour on the brainstem. He didn't regain consciousness from the surgery and died slowly after all the machines were switched off. Only fifty-three when he died, Gerd was the son who'd stayed at home. He'd married, had children, taken over the family business, been bankrupted and been divorced... but he had been a thoughtful and caring son to his ageing parents, and they, in turn, had come to depend on him, especially once his father's Alzheimer's had become apparent.

From the church on the village square it's almost a kilometre to the cemetery; the coffin, pushed on a gurney behind the thurible-swinging, prayer-reciting priest through the mid-September afternoon, arrived at the graveside before the square had emptied. We, the family and the priest, waited some fifteen minutes at the open grave, and still the funeral procession thronged into the well-ordered memorial garden, which surely kept at least one flower shop in business all year round. I peered into the hole, and wished that the whole process of German Roman Catholic funeral rites could be speeded up. Jupp's mother looked both frail and haggard clinging to her demented husband's arm and Gerd's twenty-something children, pale and red-eyed, seemed bewildered. I wondered if all the roses on the graves around us had been on 'special offer', whether they were *Fairtrade,* and whether visiting the dead of this village had become a morbid fixation... there was not a single pot of withered flowers – so synonymous with my experience of Welsh graveyards – anywhere to be seen, and everything seemed colour-coded; if September was red roses, what might October demand? I thought, too, about the hundred or so young men, mainly deserters, who were executed in this tranquil field, in the shadow of the Nazis' retreat; there's no plaque to remember them by... no rose of any colour.

Jupp had been in Germany almost a fortnight by the day of the funeral; I flew in just for two nights. Before the wake, the previous evening, we looked at the house his parents had built as their first family home. It had been rented out for more than forty years; the Korsten's pension was in property. Because of Ernst-Peter's Alzheimer's, all the properties had been neglected for some years and each had grown old with them without much care and attention. When the tenancy on the house had ended, some months before, there was much that needed to be done to make it habitable again... but nothing had been initiated. The place was filthy, dark and very 'sixties' – with no redeeming retro features... but we could make it into a comfortable home – and in the field behind the house there were alpacas and kangaroos, which were fun to watch. The morning before the funeral we opened a bank account, arranged telephone and Wi-Fi connections and registered with a health insurance company. Our move, just less than a year after Britain voted to leave the EU, was surprisingly smooth.

We fell in love in English... we'd forged our relationship over decades in English... so, in the same way that we found it difficult to speak Welsh together after Jupp had spent some weeks at Nant Gwrtheyrn when we first moved to Wales from Liverpool, shifting to German in our home life proved impossible in the first months. My grasp of the language was rudimentary and so many of the conversations we were having left no room for misunderstandings. His father's deterioration, and the care we might offer at any particular time, were daily discussions, as was his mother's inability to cope in some situations.

In the first weeks we were taken aback by the bureaucracy that invades every-day life. We arrived in Effeld in the early hours of a Saturday morning, so first thing on Monday we had to register our residence at the town hall.

"You're in a Civil Partnership?" The woman who asks the question is friendly enough. I'm amazed that she can type on her keyboard with such long and elaborately decorated fingernails.

"We're married," Jupp says.

"That's not possible," she responds. "It's not legal in this country."

"We were married in Wales," Jupp insists, and I wonder if we'll have to go through the whole rigmarole of how we were 'converted' after the law changed in 2013, which made provision for those who'd been Civilly Partnered to gain marriage status... and why, therefore, our marriage certificate is back dated to the date of our original Civil Partnership in April 2006.

"Well, your marriage isn't recognised in this country so there's no box on the form that I can fill in," she insists.

I had enough German to understand what she was saying, but not enough to express my outrage at a civil servant in an EU country telling us that our marriage wasn't recognised by the state.

"I'll put a tick in the Civil Partnership box," she offers.

"But then your official registration of us as a couple will be false, because we are married," Jupp asserts.

"It doesn't matter," she says dismissively. "It means the same thing."

"No, it's not the same thing," Jupp persists. "We are married."

"There's no box for that," she says.

"I have our marriage certificate—."

"There's no box," she interrupts, impatience in her tone and dismissing the certificate with a swipe of her hand. "There's no box."

Jupp folds our marriage certificate with some deliberation and coaxes it back into the envelope.

"I'm very surprised that you are content to have an inaccurate registration record—."

"I can't help it that there's no box," she interrupts again. "We need to fill in the remaining details; I don't have all day."

So we were falsely registered.

We had some interesting dialogue, too, with our health insurance company, especially in the first months, which took a lot of time and energy. They couldn't understand how we were funding our life in Germany as neither of us had any regular income in the country, my pension being paid in Britain, taxed in Britain and paid into a British bank account. Their regimented forms asked no questions about capital – we had transferred much of the proceeds from the sale of our house to our bank account in Germany and we certainly had enough to fund our life for many years to come – but they just wanted details of our monthly income; with a dash through the monthly income box they had no clear idea how much to charge us for our healthcare package and after many letters and telephone calls they put us on the minimum payments.

There were cultural differences too that called for some patience and re-adjustment; the dog tax, and why we had to pay more than double for a second dog, vexed us for some weeks. We get nothing for it, of course – no dog wardens, no poo-bags or bins to put them into – indeed, I quickly came to believe that because people have to pay so much, every year, to own a dog, their resentment is expressed by letting their dogs foul at will. Dog shit's a problem. But there's a paradox too; most of the lawns and flower borders have been stripped out of Effeld's front plots and replaced with ugly 'stone gardens'... chippings, pebbles, rocks of every colour and shape, laid in checkerboard patterns, yin and yang symbols, concentric circles – all to save time. And what do so many Germans do with the time they've saved? They spend Saturday morning on their knees scraping the moss and the weeds from between the paving stones so that the pavement in front of their house is... a pristine plinth for a dog shit sculpture.

There are times of the day when you can use noisy machinery and there are times when you can't. Hanging out laundry on a Sunday is frowned upon – but then, few homes have a clothes line; the electric tumble dryer made clothes lines obsolete a long time ago. Shops are closed on a Saturday afternoon – and all day Sunday. The work day begins at 7:30 – so we might get an appointment at the dentist or the doctor before eight in the morning and we often receive phone calls between half seven and eight... just as we are waking up to the morning news.

I've become fascinated by the travel advisories on the radio in the mornings. We live in North Rhine-Westphalia, the most populated German state – almost 18 million people in an area a bit bigger than Wales – with a number of large cities and industrial conurbations. The travel news usually begins, in a very understated manner, with a statement about the state-wide traffic jams: 'This morning there are... 473 kilometres of traffic jams; 396 kilometres of traffic jams; 242 kilometres... 197 kilometres... 583 kilometres... which is then followed, for two or three minutes... or longer, by the list of particular snarl-ups and the estimated time it will take to negotiate the gridlock. Of course, there are no speed limits on German *Autobahnen* – drive as fast as you like... but just don't get caught up in the congestion if you want to arrive at your destination in reasonable time! And drive as close as you can to the vehicle in front of you... and don't use your indicators, especially when coming off a roundabout. On minor roads there are no central cat's eyes, though the edge of the carriageway is marked. As someone who learned to drive on narrow Welsh roads edged with irregular dry stone walls, I always positioned my car towards the central edge of the lane; without cat's eyes, that's impossible here and I find driving at night disorientating.

At the end of our street there's a track that leads into an asparagus field. A Dutch enterprise manages this plot and every day, during the short, eight week season, a bus brings some fifty workers to dig up the treasure. Beyond this field is the lake – where our Welsh sheepdogs, Wash and Nel, have discovered that swimming after ducks is as much fun as dancing with seagulls on Dyffryn beach (but they don't mess with the Canada Geese) – and then the forest, where the smells of deer and wild boar send Nel dashing. Then you're in the Netherlands. There's no border control, of course; we're in the European Union, but all along the edge, if you look closely enough, you can see the legacy of history – tall concrete border posts like mythic standing stones, long grassy embankments that offered some shelter to those in the trenches during wars and even ancient earthworks marking out the boundaries of long forgotten territories. Where the main road crosses this edge, there's a Croatian restaurant in the old German customs building and an ice cream parlour in what housed the Dutch border controllers.

The countryside around the village is tick paradise. We check ourselves and the dogs every day. Wash, who loves being stroked and petted, will sometimes pull my hand back with his paw until I find the tick that I've missed... which makes me think that they must be irritating, if not painful. Nel, who's never been very relaxed, presents a challenge in the search for these bloated blood-suckers. On the days when she growls and even snarls as we run our fingers through the hair on her chest and belly the odd one or two are missed – and then we find bladders of blood the size of a pea around the yard and in her bed... or on the Persian carpet in the lounge!

Ernst-Peter, my father-in-law, always had dogs; he was a hunter before his guns had to be removed from the gun cabinet in his hunting room because of the Alzheimer's. He's good at finding the ticks on Wash, but Nel seems to sense his otherness and is unfriendly towards him. Walking in the forest one day he suddenly became animated – our dogs, running through the trees, triggering a memory. He explained, in some gruesome detail, how he trained his hunting dogs; he would drag a hare that he'd shot through the forest, setting a trail, and then release his beloved *Deutsche Langhaar* (always German Pointers) to snoop it out. As much as we both abhor the whole idea of hunting for sport, that our dogs took Ernst-Peter back to some day in his lost past brought a smile to our faces. We smiled, too, when he took Jutta's hand and led her off to dance to the Dutch crooner who was entertaining a small crowd at one of our local pubs. Ernst-Peter is not sure who she is now – sometimes his daughter, his wife… or just 'Jutta'. Sixties ballads on a lazy bank-holiday afternoon in a Dutch beer garden clearly brought back his happy feet and they swirled and glided to *Delilah* and *Green, green grass of home* sung in what seemed to be the local dialect.

As my own familiarity with today's standard German language – *Hochdeutsch* – increases, I realize that Ernst-Peter speaks mostly *Effelder Platt*. To call this a 'local dialect' somehow diminishes it, unless we understand dialect to mean 'a particular form of a language which is peculiar to a specific region or social group'. *Effelder Platt* has more in common with Limburgish – a widely spoken variant of old Dutch – than it does with *Hochdeutsch*. In all the towns and villages over the edge in the Netherlands and Belgium the every-day spoken language is Limburgish and some 1.6 million people consider it their mother tongue. Limburgish was first recorded in the eleventh century and is still recognised as an official minority language by both Belgium and the Netherlands. However, its widely spoken German variant goes unrecognised by the German national government and no official record of the number of speakers within Germany exists.

We walk over the edge to the watermill – *die Gitstapper Mühle* – three or four times a week… it's about Jutta's limit – as long as she has her Nordic walking sticks. In 1377 someone decided that the small stream, the *Rothenbach* (Red Stream or *Roode Beek* in Limburgish) would be an ideal power source for a grain mill. Not until the Congress of Vienna in 1815 did the stream become a border, marking an edge between nation states. The restaurant and beer garden at the mill are popular with walkers and cyclists, and whilst their coffee isn't the best in the area, it's worth the walk through the forest for their rice and apricot flan. As children, my brother and I would fight for the left-over rice pudding, still in the dish in which it had been baked. Tony liked the slightly scorched skin and to this day I can devour thick (almost solid) cold rice pudding with relish. The mill's flan would be a great 'technical challenge' on Bake-Off. The base is a sweet, enriched yeast dough, rolled thinly and baked blind like a pastry case. This is then filled with rice pudding – with added egg yolks and cream – and baked until the rice mixture has set. When cooled, stewed apricots are layered over the rice and the confection is topped with whipped cream. I'm reliably informed that the sincerest compliment that can be offered to a cook in the Netherlands is *Alsof er een engeltje over je tong piest*. Someone, of course, may be pulling my leg – but the taste of *Gitstapper Mühle's* rice and apricot flan 'is like a little angel peeing on your tongue'.

I'm asked often if I'm homesick for Wales. Of course, I miss people... but I've always believed, as someone whose glass hasn't been half empty for decades, that contentment comes from inside, and that a person with a happy temperament will be happy wherever they find themselves. That Wales voted to leave the EU is a bitter disappointment to me and that makes it easier; in those rare moments of nostalgic wallowing that can seep in at the oddest times, I remind myself that whatever Wales I hanker for, it is not the Wales which emerged that day in June 2016.

We get questioning looks when we mention Brexit; we get shrugged shoulders and hands lifted into the air... we get heads shaking in disbelief. Mention Boris and mostly people laugh and ask how such a buffoon can become so influential in British politics. No one has ever heard of Gove and Theresa May's name draws the lines of derision across people's faces. Mostly, folk here don't grasp the concept of a soft or hard Brexit – doesn't leave mean exactly that? If you choose to leave a club you don't negotiate what privileges of club membership you might retain... do you? We listen to the BBC news, and read what friends from Britain post on social media – and sometimes we despair. For a long time, not much about Brexit was reported in the German media – though the farcical chaos of the weeks leading up to the UK's supposed departure at the end of March 2019 did feature most evenings on the news, when I got the sense that the newsreaders were having difficulty keeping a straight face. Frankly, I believe most Germans are genuinely sad about Brexit – but life here goes on and Britain's departure will have little long-term impact on everyday life.

2

Rooms with Views

Ernst-Peter would occasionally accompany me to walk the dogs. In the first weeks I came to realise that we had a lot in common: our brains weren't wired for the moment. My grasp of the language often faltered... by the time I'd worked out what was being said to me and constructed my response the moment had passed. As someone who likes to talk, hear stories and tell stories, this caused me profound frustration. With time, practice and effort my competence would, of course, improve. There was little chance that Ernst-Peter would regain his competence; Alzheimer's is cruel in any language.

He loved the dogs; he'd throw sticks for them and feel around their ears for ticks – and he'd laugh a lot at Nel's playfulness. Their names he couldn't grasp; they were 'the black one' and 'the brown one'. With Ernst-Peter we didn't walk too far; sometimes he just wanted to walk around the block – which meant passing the field with the alpacas and the kangaroos; they always surprised him – and surprised the dogs. Some days we'd walk to the café by the watermill in The Netherlands for a coffee or a beer, and rice flan with cherries, Ernst-Peter's favourite... or along the lake as far as the turtles – they were always in the same spot, basking in the sunshine on a partly submerged tree trunk. Nel would sit on the bank and look inquisitively at them; Wash would get confused when they slipped from their perch into the water and disappeared... Ernst-Peter's fascination with them was a joy to see, but being with him often made me think about my mother's last demented years.

I was always unsettled when she spoke directly with me in English. We'd always spoken Welsh together, unless we were in monoglot English company. Of course, she was fluent in both languages, but in English she'd speak with a pretentious telephone voice, pronouncing local people's names and the near-by villages in a bastard idiom. Mindful that the gerontologist had advised us not to contradict her, or to do too much reality testing, which would merely exacerbate her confusion and make her more agitated, we'd just chat... about the weather, or how the pears that had mysteriously appeared in the fruit bowl were still too hard... that the grape skins on the red grapes were tougher than those of the green – although she preferred the red... or that Terry had been sitting with her – though he never said a word. Often she'd try to describe how dark the days were and how bright the nights could be, and for a while this had me baffled... until one day it dawned on me that her circadian rhythms were confounded by the oxygen-starved neurons, so typical of vascular dementia. Just once, in one of the frequent lulls of our fragmented conversations, I asked her why we weren't speaking Welsh… and her watery, red-rimmed eyes fixed me in a probing stare, as if she was searching for some right answer that had escaped her.

"Terry hasn't come home yet," she says, even before a hello.

I dislike the playing-along-make-believe but that was the doctor's advice.

"Has he been gone a long time?" I ask.

She says he went to work, as usual. Something has spilled down the front of her blouse, a violent red colour. I suggest that I help her change into a clean top. She insists that it's not necessary.

"Do you think he's alright?" she asks.

I assure her that Terry's probably still at work and suggest again that we change her blouse… so that she'll look nice when he returns. After just a moment's pause, she concedes. Her arthritis-gnarled fingers fumble with the delicate mother-of-pearl buttons, and she snags a hangnail on the sheer gauze fabric.

"It's stuck," she says, tugging at the caught thread.

I free her finger from the pulled strand of cotton and open each button, explaining that I'll trim her fingernails after changing her blouse. She's wearing neither a vest nor a brassiere and seeing her wizened, blue-veined breasts, I feel suddenly vulnerable... as if I'm doing something inappropriate – wrong, even... something too personal for a son to do for his mother. My sense of unease stretches into my mother's indecision about which blouse to wear and in those moments of discomfort I wonder what other 'personal things' I might eventually need to do for her... and whether I'll be able to do them.

I cut and file her fingernails every fortnight – except those times when she refuses to let me – and I massage lavender hand cream into her tissue-paper-thin skin, which she likes because the cream isn't too greasy. The NHS chiropodist sees to her feet every month... except when she doesn't turn up; the knotted toes and the fungal nails are beyond my comfort zone. Once, when the chiropodist failed to show for a third time, I paid for a private podiatrist; he did a lot of tut-tutting at the state of Megan's feet and recommended new slippers at least every month. "...because slippers, worn all day, every day, harbour fungal spores." I buy two new pairs of slippers, so that one pair can always be put in the washing machine with my trainers. Megan refuses to wear either pair... she even retrieves the manky ones from the bin after I leave.

"You look nice now," I say, putting the clippers and file back in her vanity case. "Let me brush your hair for when Terry comes back."

She holds my gaze, her eyes questioning.

"Who's Terry? Which one is he?"

She turns the pages of the dog-eared photograph album. "They're all black and white," she mutters.

I urge her to look more carefully.

"Oh... you've been to a wedding... they'd look nicer in colour."

I ask if she recognises anyone in the pictures.

"No," she says, and pushes the album away.

I turn the pages to the photograph of the bride and groom with their parents, best man and maid of honour. "You know who these are, don't you?" I say, encouraging her to look again.

"Is that me?" she says, pointing at the bride after some consideration.

"Yes, it's you... sixty years ago today... when you got married."

"Oh," she says, with a quizzical tone and the merest shake of her head. She looks again at the photograph and she smiles. "I've still got that costume... it's hanging in the wardrobe."

I smile, grateful that perhaps she's recognised something in the picture.

"Why didn't you wear a white wedding dress?" I ask.

"I don't think I've ever been married," she says.

"This is you and Terry on your wedding day," I assure her, pointing at the young bride and groom.

"He was a handsome boy," she says. "She was a lucky girl, whoever she is."

"It's you, Mam," I say, reaching for the more recent photograph of Terry from the vitrine that holds the few ornaments brought from her own home. Pointing at my father's image I say, "You were married to him for forty-nine years."

She looks at the photo of Terry, taken by the lilac tree in the garden the spring before he died. "I remember now," she says, "I've been meaning to ask you for ages... who is he? Why is his picture on there?"

One day I ask the manager about the bruises on Megan's arms. The manager explains that she had fallen in the toilet and 'the girls' had to 'manhandle' her out of the narrow cubicle. I ask Megan if she remembers falling in the toilet. She can't remember. After a long time staring out of the window as if I weren't there, she says, rubbing the bruises on her arms, "Why do you keep coming to see me?" I'm grateful, at least, that she seems to know me from day to day.

"Because you're my mother," I say. "And that's what sons do... visit their mother."

She looks out of the window again... and her knees begin to shake... and her fingers tangle...

"Why do you try to confuse me all the time?" she blurts. "I've only got two boys, and they're in school today... so

don't you come here again saying that I'm your mother...
go away, now!"

"Yes, you have got two boys, Mam. Tony and me...."

"They're in school today... now, go away and stop
making trouble for me."

I talked with the doctor again after that incident because I
needed to understand. She explained that Megan probably
spent her days in a series of locked rooms. She might wake
up in her bedroom in Parkfield, the house where she worked
as a maid, and it would be 1945. Everything about that
room, and the household where she lived, would be alive
to her, and of course, she'd be single and childless. Or it
could be the kitchen of her new marital home in 1952...
or the lounge in the family home in 1966 with two young
boys around her... such were the common symptoms of
her type of dementia. "So if she's locked in time and space
when you're a boy of twelve," the doctor says, "she won't
recognise a fifty-something grey-haired man as her son."

Megan sits with a large, half-empty box of chocolates on
her lap and chocolate goo in the corners of her mouth.
No, she has no idea who brought them. I go back to the
reception desk and check the comings and goings in the
book since my visit the day before and I make out my
Uncle John's signature. Back in her room I ask how long
her brother had stayed. She hasn't seen her brother for a

long time... he's still at sea. I trawl my memory to recall whether Uncle John has ever been in the navy.

"Do you want me to bring you chocolates sometimes, instead of pears or grapes?"

"*Milk Tray*," she says, and smiles. "'All because the lady loves *Milk Tray*.'"

My heart skips a beat.

"You remember how we used to sing along to all the TV ads," I say.

She laughs.

"'*Bird's Eye* peas, fresh as the morning, fresh as the morning when the pods went pop,'" she sings, and laughs, and laughs.

"Do you remember the one for *Toblerone*?"

I sing the jingle and she joins in. After laughing some more she says, "I used to sing these with my youngest."

"With John," I say, remembering what the doctor had said about her not recognising a middle aged man with greying hair as her son.

"Yes, with John," she says. "I've got two boys, Tony and John. They're both doing well at school, you know."

I want for her to know that I'm John, and that Tony had travelled from Liverpool to see her only weeks previously... but we always seemed to be locked out of the rooms she was inhabiting.

"Dada brought me these chocolates," she says into my thoughts.

And I reflect on how much my Uncle John, in his old age, has come to resemble his own father – my maternal grandfather.

"Mrs Thomas has come to see you," I say, ushering the social worker into her room. "She wants to talk to you about how you're being looked after."

The social worker speaks in Welsh and Megan answers in English... a series of simple questions to ascertain whether she's competent to attend the Care Review. Yes, she likes living there... it's a lovely hotel, and she never has to pay in the restaurant – but she always takes her purse. No, she's not married – never has been. Children? Yes, she's got two – a girl and a boy: she names them without hesitation – Una and Timothy. And how old is she? A smile... eyes searching... "Very old," she says, and laughs. Mrs Thomas writes on the pro forma in the file on her knee: *Megan Jones isn't orientated in time or place and has little sense of her own history. This review will be conducted with her son, John Sam Jones.*

In the office, where the Care Review takes place with the manager and one of the care assistants, the social worker asks about the boy and girl, Timothy and Una.

"They're the two children she helped to bring up when she went into service with the Parry family in Parkfield in 1944," I say.

I usually walk to the care home, just twenty minutes to the other side of town... but in blustery rain, or on days when running a B&B is just too much work and I'm pushed for time, I drive. It's a warm, spring afternoon, and I'm behind with everything on my list.

"I'm ready to go," she says in Welsh, even before I sit down.

I glance at my watch and figure I can spare half an hour.

"You saw me park the car, did you? Come on then, let's go and sit at the end of the prom and have an ice-cream."

She reaches forward and takes my hand. "Yn barod i fynd... Ready to... go... you know?"

Partly distracted by the list in my mind's eye, and second-guessing myself about the time it would take to go for ice-cream, I say, "You don't want to go out in the car?"

"I want to go," she says again, a pleading quality in her voice which makes me pay her more attention... and then I realize that she's in the moment... that we're in the same room.

"Where do you want to go, Mam?"

"To heaven," she says.

I feel as if someone has punched me in the stomach.

"You can go to heaven," I venture, "...but only when God's ready for you... not before."

"Well, I'm ready, my *Siwgwr Aur*... this is no life for me."

My thoughts spill over... she's recognised me... she's called me by one of her oft used diminutives... she's aware... my heart is breaking... there are things on this damn list that have to be done today.

"Oh, Mam —," I bite my tongue hard to stop the tears.

"This is no life, John," she says. "The kindest thing you could do for me would be to smother me with that pillow."

"I can't do that for you, Mam... I'd be sent to gaol."

"Yes...," she says, releasing my hand and slouching back into her chair.

We sit opposite one another, a gaping gash of unspokenness between us. Perhaps I can take the pillow... perhaps that's the most loving thing I can do for her....

"You'd better go if you can't help me," she says.

Out in the car I shake with tears and upset... and I hope that the next time I see her she'll be away in cloud-cuckoo land... locked in one of her rooms.

The tasks on my list occupy me for the remainder of the afternoon. Later, after talking with Tony on the phone, I contact Megan's GP and relate our conversation about what I supposed was assisted suicide. The doctor says she'll be happy to discuss the possibility of a trip to a clinic in Switzerland... and in the meantime she'll write out a script for an antidepressant which might help lift Megan's mood.

I sit for a while and watch her sleep. I notice the dried detritus of a spill on the lace ruffle of her nightdress and the purple blotch, the size of a two-pence piece, in the fold of her elbow... where the community nurse must have taken blood again. The skin on her inner forearm has a translucent quality, the veins raised and baby-blue. Her breathing is consistent, easy somehow, showing no trace of the emphysema nurtured by six decades of nicotine addiction – with its incumbent damage to her airways and arteries. I smile to myself when I remember how, many decades before – when I was a student and she was worried about cannabis, LSD and heroin – I'd challenged her prejudices about 'drug addicts' by suggesting she hold up a mirror when she had a cigarette in her mouth. Unused to such actuality, she'd responded by blanking me for the rest of that day. I listen intently to her breathing and I'm curious about the rhythm, which seems too shallow for deep sleep... and I notice the movements of her eyes behind the closed lids – which seem too intentional, somehow.

"Are you awake?" I ask.

Her eyes still, and there's almost an imperceptible falter in the measure of her breaths.

"I'm sorry if I woke you up," I say.

"I'm sleeping... go away," she says, eyes now more tightly shut, her sunken cheeks almost puffed.

"It's time for lunch," I say. "Shall I help you dress and sit with you in the dining room?"

"It's the middle of the night," she says. "I'm sleeping... go away."

For the next three days, when I visit, she's 'sleeping'.

She's sitting next to her bed in her nightdress, her red woollen coat over her shoulders, the bed stripped to the pressure relieving spenco mattress.

"How did you find me?" she asks.

"Your name is on the door," I say, not really sure what else to say until I get more of a sense of what's happening with her.

"I don't know why they've left me here," she says. "I want to go back to my little house."

"This is your room."

"But look at it," she says, pointing at the bed. "It's nobody's... there's no bed... and I've just been dumped here in my coat... am I waiting for something?"

"I think someone's in the middle of making up a nice, clean bed for you... I'll see if I can find one of the girls."

In the office, the manager says that they got Megan up for breakfast... and then had taken her bed linen away so that she couldn't go back to bed.

"Has anyone looked in on her?" I ask. "She's sitting in her nightdress and her coat, totally unsettled."

"She wouldn't get dressed this morning so one of the girls put her coat over her shoulders so she wouldn't be cold."

"And you obviously think that this is an appropriate way to deal with a demented old lady—."

"I've told you before, John... your mother can be very difficult," the manager cuts in. "We need for her to follow our routine as much as possible, but when she sleeps all day, and then wanders the corridors at night causing problems for the night staff... it's difficult for us. And if she's in bed at meal times it's more work – to make up a tray and take it to her room."

"I understand that this is a care home, not a nursing home," I say after a few deep breaths to subdue my anger. "I understand, too, that you have a daily routine, and that there is an expectation that the residents fall in with that routine... but my mother is here because her dementia means that she can't look after herself... her dementia makes her behave in ways that won't always seem rational... or fit your routine. It isn't a month since you sat in on her Care Review with the social worker and then you made out that everything was sweetness and light... you didn't even mention that she can be aggressive with your staff... and now you seem to be saying she's really problematic."

The manager straightens her back and pushes out her ample bosom, as though she's about to bring the conversation to an end.

"I haven't finished yet," I say. "If you feel you can't look after my mother in a civilised way then please call another Care Review... perhaps she's ready to move to a nursing home. But now... I'd like her bed made up... immediately, and I don't want anything like this to happen again – for as long as she remains here. I'll stay until that's been done. And... before I leave your office, I'd like you to telephone your immediate line manager and explain what has happened – and then hand me the phone so that I can speak with her... or him, as the case may be. Oh... and I'd like one of your complaint forms... for official complaints!"

"I've got two of my day staff on sick leave..." the manager begins, no longer holding my gaze, her chest deflated.

"Managing staff rotas... and managing the appropriate care of your residents is, I would suppose, part of your day-to-day responsibility."

"...and we're just about to serve lunch, so there's no one free to make up the bed."

"Well then, perhaps you can do it, after you've made that phone call to your manager."

We both speak with the area care manager. She concedes nothing on the phone as to the appropriateness of the events I describe, but invites me to put in a written complaint. Then she asks to be handed back to the home manager – who, after no more than a minute, puts the receiver in the cradle and says she'll go and make up Megan's bed.

In the corridor we find a disorientated woman in a red woollen coat, flustered... panicky even, because she can't find her room.

The phone rings just after eight in the morning. We're serving breakfast to six guests who've all come down together. The manager of the care home tells Jupp that Megan's been whisked off to the hospital in Bangor. I come to the phone and ask what happened... why they called the ambulance.

"She was struggling for breath and the agency nurse thought it best," she says.

"But she always struggles for breath," I say. "Isn't it written in her notes that you should call me if she's unwell at night? Isn't that what we agreed at the last Care Review?"

"Perhaps, if the regular night staff had been on... someone who knows Megan—."

"What time did the ambulance take her?"

I feel my anxiety rising; my mother will be completely lost in a big, general hospital.

"A couple of hours ago."

"And nobody went with her... and nobody thought to phone me."

"Well, as I said, we had a new agency nurse on last night."

I hung up the phone before my anger got the better of me. I talk with someone at the hospital in Bangor after being put on hold for what seems an age.

"She's still in A&E," the voice says. "She's on oxygen, and we're waiting for her to be seen by a doctor... then we can decide whether she needs to be admitted or sent back home."

I explain something of her circumstances... that she probably doesn't know her own name, or date of birth... I say I'll be there as soon as I can and leave Jupp to manage the three room turn around. When I arrive, she's lying on a trolley in a small, curtained off 'cubicle', still waiting to see a doctor. She's in her nightdress and dressing gown, and I chide myself for not having the presence of mind before leaving home to bring her some warm clothes.

"Who are you?" she asks, when I go to take her hand.

"Are you breathing better... with that oxygen?"

"I always struggle with my breathing," she says.

With a swipe of an arm the curtain parts and a white-coated doctor comes to her side. "Megan Jones?" she asks.

I smile at the doctor, but say nothing. I want her to see for herself how confused Megan is.

"Are you Megan Lloyd Jones?" the doctor asks again.

Megan looks blank at the doctor and I wonder whether it's just that she hasn't heard her over the clamour beyond the curtains. The doctor turns to me; "And you are...?"

"John, Megan's son, though most of the time she doesn't know it."

"Alzheimer's?" the doctor quizzes.

"Smoking-related vascular dementia," I say.

"So, she has COPD," the doctor says, half a question, half an assertion.

"Yes," I say. "But I'm never sure what that acronym stands for... emphysema."

"Chronic obstructive pulmonary disease," the doctor says. "It covers a wide range of pulmonary conditions." She writes something on the uppermost sheet of a wodge of paperwork. "So you called the ambulance because her breathing got much worse?"

"Megan lives in a care home and last night they had staff on who don't know her, so it seems they panicked a bit."

The doctor moves towards Megan.

"I need to listen to your chest, Mrs Jones," she says. "Can we sit you up?"

She is gentle and respectful with her, and very patient.

"I don't think there's any infection," she says after probing Megan's chest and back with the stethoscope. "False alarm, I think," she says to me.

"I can take her home then?"

"Yes," the doctor says.

I find a spare wheelchair and wheel her to the tea room. She has two pieces of toast with raspberry jam... and then there's another stain on the lace ruffle of her nightdress. The tea is too hot, in a paper cup that nestles into a plastic handle... which is difficult for her to manage with her mangled fingers. I ask the man behind the serving counter for a straw, and when the tea has cooled she seems to enjoy it.

"I need the toilet," she says, as I wheel her towards the

main exit and the vast car park beyond. I feel uneasy... that the next few minutes will take me way beyond my comfort zone. Parking the wheelchair outside the 'Ladies', I wonder if she'll manage on her own.

"Do you need some help?" a disembodied voice asks.

I turn to see a nurse, dressed in a jacket with a bag over her shoulder, either just arriving for a shift, or just leaving.

"That would be great," I say.

It's already lunchtime when we arrive back at the care home. I say that I'll sit with her while she has her lunch. She wants to get dressed first... that nice mauve suit.

As I pull into the car park I see my Uncle John, still handsome and lithe at eighty, scurrying through the drizzle towards the entrance of the care home. Without thinking, I tap the horn and wave. Uncle John recognises me immediately and points at the door, a gesture I interpret as *I'll meet you in the foyer*.

We shake hands and exchange tads of news... Auntie Nesta has had the flu... one of the great-grandchildren came off her bike and has broken her wrist. I'm mindful that I should have been in touch with Uncle John before now – he's so faithful to his sister, visiting every week... and I want to ask about the navy.

"I can come and see Megan later," I say to him. "It seems pointless for both of us to sit with her. Will you call in for a cup of tea on your way home?"

"Alright then," Uncle John says. "I don't usually spend more than twenty minutes with your mam... how is she?"

"Up and down," I say... not really sure what to say. "Does she speak Welsh with you?"

"Funny you should say that," he says. "I talk in Welsh and she answers in English."

"But she does know who you are, does she?"

"Well... I'm not sure. She's called me Dada more than once."

"Well... you do look a lot like *Taid*."

"He had a lot more hair than me," Uncle John says, patting his bald patch, laughing.

"So... I'll see you in – what? About an hour?"

Uncle John nods. "Have you got any of that fruitcake," he asks. "The one you said was Megan's recipe?"

"Yes... and a Victoria sandwich," I say, recalling how much Uncle John likes cake.

Within the hour we're sitting in the lounge at Dros y Dŵr, with its view across the Mawddach to Cadair Idris, drinking tea and eating cake.

"Megan thought I was Dada again today," Uncle John says.

I sketch the doctor's theory about her being locked in rooms in different times and Uncle John seems to accept the plausibility of it all.

"Was she up and dressed?"

"Yes, she looked real tidy. She wanted to know if I'd been to Parkfield, to see Mr Parry."

"She's pre-nineteen-sixty then."

"It's that long since old Mr Parry died, is it?" Uncle John says, shaking his head.

"And how did she seem today?" I ask.

"She had plenty to say... she'd been to Chester for the day with Mrs Parry... shopping."

"She seems quite content when she's wrapped up in her past," I say. "But sometimes she's lucid...." I wonder whether to tell him about her plea to be suffocated with the pillow.

"Oh... this dementia is very cruel... it's very hard for you, John *bach*."

"It's hard for all of us, Uncle John."

There's an awkwardness between us... then, eyeing the plate of cakes, Uncle John says that the fruitcake is very good.

"Were you ever in the navy?" I ask, gesturing him to help himself.

"No," Uncle John says, looking puzzled and taking another slice of the fruitcake. "I only caught the tail end of National Service... and that's how I went into the Forestry Commission. I was never in the armed forces."

"It was just something Mam said. You'd been there one day – with chocolates... I asked her if they were from you but she said it was her dada that had brought them... and that her brother was still at sea."

"Mixing me up with Teddy," Uncle John says.

"Who's Teddy?"

"Oh... she never told you about Edward?"

I shrug.

"It will be a bit of a surprise then... Teddy is... was our half-brother."

"I didn't know that *Nain* had been married before."

"Well, no... she wasn't married. She had a child when she was in service in Aberystwyth – probably the man of the house, thinking he'd paid for that service too... but who knows? To her credit, she kept the baby... came home and looked after him."

"So why do you think Megan never told us?"

"It all got a bit messy, John *bach*," Uncle John continues... "When Mama met Dada, he would only marry her if she gave up the boy. Think about it – it's the mid-nineteen-twenties, she's a single mother, she meets a man who will marry her and 'make her respectable'... but she has to give up Edward."

"I can't believe nobody told us this," I say.

"Well, it doesn't put either of your grandparents in a very good light," Uncle John ventures. "One of Mama's maiden aunts took Edward and Dada eventually agreed that he could come and see his mother, but only when Dada wasn't home... and Teddy used to come, most days, after school... so we grew up with him – but because we were just children we never thought to ask about the arrangements."

"We can't judge people today for the hard choices they had to make eighty-odd years ago," I say.

"You're right, of course, but when your mother and I, and our sisters became adults and started families of our own we decided not to tell our children about Ted. He'd disappeared, somehow, after the War... nobody knew where he was, so we just thought it was better not to say anything. I only told my own children when they were adults."

"What do you mean, he disappeared?"

"It's only in the last years I found out what happened to him," Uncle John says. "Just after the War he met and fell in love with a girl from a – well, 'posh' family; I think her father was a solicitor... or a vet. Ted was afraid that if Elizabeth, and her family, knew that he was illegitimate they'd find him unacceptable. In the War, lots of people lost everything, so Teddy reinvented himself as one of the survivors whose home and family had been destroyed in a bombing raid... and once he'd adopted that story there was no going back."

"It's like something from a novel," I say.

"Teddy and Elizabeth had three children... and there are grandchildren and great-grandchildren."

"So how did you find out?"

"One of his sons... curious I suppose... researching the family tree – and he got a copy of Ted's birth certificate. Well, Blodwen George wasn't such a common name and he then found her marriage certificate to Dada and then all our birth certificates – your mother, me, our sisters... so then it wasn't so difficult for him to find us."

"Are you in touch with them?"

"Teddy and Elizabeth are dead by now, but we get a Christmas card from one of their boys; they're down on the south coast, Exeter I think."

After Uncle John left, I found myself reflecting once again on family secrets, and how what's left out of the family saga is sometimes what might have made all the difference.

"I'm glad you've come," she says, standing at the window of her room, looking fretful. "I can't get over to Parkfield today because both these boys have got the measles. Will you go and see that Mr Parry gets his dinner?"

"I'm a bit pushed for time," I say.

"I made a beef casserole for them yesterday," she says. "You just need to see that it's warmed up for him when he comes in from the smithy."

"Here are your magazines," I say, thinking I'll distract her. "And there's a supplement, look... *Ten Summer Romances*."

"Oh, that's lovely," she says, "but I haven't got time to read them today... Oh..." She looks around the room and after a moment she says, "Not today, I'm too busy; I've got the hall, stairs and landing in Parkfield to clean and the floor tiles in the hall could do with a polish... and then I'm off with Jean, on the train back to Birmingham."

"I thought you couldn't get to Parkfield today... didn't you say that the boys have got the measles?"

"Which boys?"

"I must have misunderstood," I say, trying not to confuse her. "So, you're going to Birmingham with Jean?"

"I'm living in Birmingham now, with Jean – at her auntie's house."

"I never knew you'd lived in Birmingham," I say.

"Girls... when they're in trouble... they get sent away," she says in a whisper.

"So, Jean's having a baby?" I say – curious... but recalling the yellowing photograph of Jean and Alan's grand, white wedding in one of our family albums, and the photograph of my parent's 'immediate family only' marriage, Megan in a dark, formal 'costume', I wondered if it was Megan who'd been expecting: another family secret?

It's a gloriously sunny afternoon and I've persuaded her to go for a short drive. Once she's settled in the front seat I ask if she'd like to go and see her brother, John.

"I haven't been to put flowers on Terry's grave for a long time," she says. We're speaking Welsh again.

"There were some nice roses in the Co-op this morning," I say. "We can stop there on the way."

"Don't you think we should put some artificial ones? I don't go so often now and artificial would last."

"I don't know where to buy artificial flowers," I say.

"That discount place," she says.

"The Pound Shop in the old chapel... is that the one you mean?

"Yes," she says. "That's the chapel where you and your brother were christened."

I turn into the high street, feeling a little unnerved that she's so lucid, and find a parking space a few hundred yards from the old chapel.

"Can you get a bit closer?" she asks. "I'd like to go in."

I curse under my breath... getting her out of the car, up the steps and into the chapel... and then back down the steps and into the car will take an age. "I don't think there's a space," I say... but then feel I'm being mean to her. I pull out into the street and drive slowly... and find a gap in the line of parked cars just to the right of the chapel door.

"I used to come here every Sunday night, you know," she says as I help her up the steps. "I couldn't go in the morning because I had to make Sunday dinner for half past twelve. There was a group of us, girls in service; we'd sit together."

"And is this the chapel where you and Dad were married?"

"Yes," she says. "Those yellow ones will do," she says,

pointing at a bunch of plastic chrysanthemums in a tub just inside the chapel door. "They'll look lovely."

It's a good fifty yards from the cemetery car park to Terry's grave.

"You know that there's room for me in there," she says as we approach.

"I thought you wanted to be cremated," I say.

"I do," she says. "And then you can put the ashes in here."

Helping me arrange the plastic chrysanthemums she says, "I hope it won't be long... I have had enough, you know."

"I know, Mam," I say.

"I pray every day you know... for God to take me. I'd do it myself if I could," she says, her voice falling away.

"We could go to one of those clinics in Geneva... if you really think you're ready."

"Geneva," she says. "Nancy and I were there once... there's a big fountain. The wind blew all the spray, like rain..." she laughs. "We got wet and had to sit on the coach in damp clothes."

"I can look into it for you—."

"I'm too old to go to Switzerland," she says. "It's too far to go on the bus and I never did like aeroplanes."

She picks at one or two of the chrysanthemums. "I won't have to come up here again... they'll do now... and perhaps the next time you come up here you'll be putting my ashes in a hole."

We walk, arm-in-arm, back to the car. I wonder if I should pursue the conversation about mercy killing... I wonder if helping her would be an act of kindness – or selfishness. At the steps by the cemetery gate she interrupts my reverie... "Where are we? What are we doing here?" she asks in English.

As we turn to pass through the gate I point back at the brash yellow chrysanthemums. "You wanted to put flowers on Dad's grave."

"Who's grave?" she asks, with emphasis on the 'who' that leaves me wondering what room she'd stepped into as we'd walked along the cemetery path.

My mother died just a few weeks before her eighty-third birthday in February 2013. Jupp, Tony and his new wife, Georgina, and I put the small tub of ashes from the crematorium into a hole dug into the grave where Terry's ashes lay with his mother, his father and his maternal grandmother... and we recited the Lord's Prayer together. The brash yellow chrysanthemums looked weather-worn. Megan's death was a blessing, and brought Tony and me more relief than grief – for hadn't we lost our mother years before? We never did find out if there was a child given up for adoption in Birmingham; the possibility was no longer a secret in the family but sometimes you question whether you need to know. A mystery, perhaps, for another generation to solve?

3

Approaching Manhood

There are fields all around Jupp's *Heimat* – Effeld. In April, when we arrived, the crop of rapeseed was too yellow to look at in the afternoon sun; I'd never noticed how much like lilac it smells, but walking on the farm track between two long fields of blossom, the scent was intoxicating and the hum of bees drowned the babble of the stream which marks the edge. There are tens of kilometres of asparagus, in earthed-up rows to stop the spears photosynthesising – some with black plastic covers, like discarded raincoats, to ensure they need harvesting only once a day; asparagus is the 'white gold' of the village and is sold on market stalls across the country at a premium. The eight-week season, from late April to late June, brings diners to the four local restaurants and booking a table is essential. There are bean plants too, they'll be ploughed-in to enrich the sandy soil... and grain fields – the crops, wheat, rye and oats, already waist-high... and pastures with cattle, their tails – like metronomes – swatting the flies. Yes, there are lots of flies. We live on *Mückenstraße... Mücken* are mosquitoes.

Jupp hasn't lived in Effeld since he was sent, as a nine-year-old, to a Roman Catholic boarding school... because first sons become priests. As that little boy of nine, everyone knew him as Juppi... and now, fifty years later, they still call him Juppi. I dislike it when adults are still called by their childhood nicknames, the same way that I dislike it when adults still call their parents Mummy and Daddy; to me it's an indication that neither the maturity of the individual, nor the maturity of the relationship between parents and adult children is acknowledged. Jutta, Jupp's mother, calls him Juppi – but then, she never really got to know him as an adult. Sometimes... often, she treats him like that nine-year-old – and sometimes he becomes the nine-year-old that he was.

When Tony and I were kids, one of our favourite Welsh language programmes on the television was *Ryan a Ronnie* – a comedy series that always ended with an episode of a spoof soap opera *Tŷ Ni* –'Our House'. Ryan Davies played the domineering mother, Ronnie Williams the 'bit of a wimp' father. They had two children (played by adults), a son, Nigel Wyn – spoilt rotten by his mother, and a daughter, Phyllis Doris – whom the mother always called a 'brazen hussy'. There were running jokes; Nigel Wyn, at some point in every episode, would call his father Will, to which the doting mother would respond *'Paid a galw Will ar dy dad, Nigel Wyn'*. A direct translation from Welsh would be 'Don't call Will on your father', and in the spirit of spoof soap opera, Tony started calling our father Terry – to which our mother immediately responded, '*Paid a galw Terry ar dy dad*', and our father echoed with 'Don't call Terry on your father', but always with a grin. And so it became a running joke between us... and not very long after, we were mostly on first name terms with Megan and Terry.

I wonder sometimes if our parents thought they were being progressive in allowing such informality, but in reality I could find little openness between us. I don't recall talking about anything much that mattered; the length of Tony's hair was a running conversation for about three years, as were the price of butter, bacon and the butcher's home-made sausages – and 'news' of people in town... but never gossip.

Believing that he had our best interests at heart, and obviously being too embarrassed to talk openly about sex with either of us, Terry bought us a copy of *Approaching Manhood – Healthy Sex for Boys*. Tony, being the oldest, read it first but said nothing... not even when I asked. What I remember from my careful reading of this slim book was that something I had already discovered to be pleasurable was called self-abuse. I looked up the word *abuse* in the dictionary and was confused.

The chapter on self-abuse described the activity as shameful and harmful, causing an array of afflictions: blindness, hairy palms, penis shrinkage and curvature, acne, low sperm count because of the wastage, physical weakness and ultimately mental illness – and if that was not enough, the self-abuser always experienced profound guilt after the event. Terry had given no invitation to talk about the contents of the book when he handed it to me... and anyway, perhaps I was the only boy in Barmouth who enjoyed 'abusing' himself, so talking to Tony didn't seem right either – and hadn't he already brushed off my questions about the book? The pleasure I got from this 'abuse' had to remain my secret.

Once a week my mother's magazine would drop through the letterbox; she subscribed to *Woman* for more than twenty years. Her friend, Jane, had three magazines a week and they always swopped. I liked the horoscopes and the knitting patterns – and I especially liked the problem pages... and it was in one of these agony aunt columns that I read about an adolescent's fantasies when he abused himself: he thought about other boys. It was the first time I came across the term homosexual. The agony aunt's advice was to seek medical advice and be referred to a psychiatrist who could help cure the problem.

Through primary school I never felt left out. I played with girls, Nerys and Carys especially; Nerys lived just a few doors away and had a huge box of old clothes under their stairs – for dressing up. We created characters and acted-out other lives in cast-off sweaters, skirts and hats. I played with boys too. Stephen Jones had been my best friend until he went off to boarding school; when he came home in the holidays it was never quite the same because I'd drifted into other friendship groups. Though I didn't care much for football, which seemed to be what most of the boys liked to do, a gang of us would play war games – cowboys and Indians in the derelict farm on the hill behind the town, British and Germans in the sand-dunes behind the quay and Robin Hood in the woods – but all that stopped when one of the lads was shot in the eye with a reed arrow from a home-made bow. He lost the eye, of course, but took much gruesome delight pulling out the gawping prosthetic orb in class – especially if we had a new student teacher.

I was going to miss Mr Roberts, one of my primary school teachers. Sometimes, when he leaned over to look at my work or help with a particular problem, I got distracted – by his smell, which was pleasantly spicy, and by the hair on his arms. I tried hard not to think about him when I abused myself. But then, my arrival at Ysgol Ardudwy in Harlech, our local secondary school, offered new experiences. We had to change out of our school uniform for rugby and gymnastics – and we had to shower at the end of the PE lessons... and puberty had been triggered in most of the boys I showered with – and on occasion, older boys would use the showers at the same time... and Mr Roberts was pushed out of my fantasies.

On the first morning at Ysgol Ardudwy we were streamed; the new school was comprehensive only in name, a grammar school and a secondary modern school thrown together some years before under one roof in a new building. I was with the children sent to the two grammar classes but many of my friends were sent to the lower ability streams, and without the companionship of those friends from primary school I remember feeling a bit lost, and a bit lonely. Of course, new friends were made, but even before half term the bullying began. First it was sissy, and *cadi-ffan*, pansy and *pansan*... but then, as the months passed, the taunts became harsher. I began, for the first time in my life, to experience other people's desire to exclude me. It wasn't something I could immediately articulate... but I recall that it made me feel ashamed. And so began a life at the periphery.

My new English teacher – another Roberts – was concerned that my reading was slow and faltering. She was also the school librarian and often spent her lunch-times in the library, so she encouraged me to join her for twenty minutes, a couple of times a week, to read something – anything – from the shelves. I don't believe I was a serious child, but I discovered *The Guardian*; the school put a copy in the staff room every day and the old copies went into the library for two weeks. After a while, I suppose learning to trust one another, Miss Roberts would point to a short article and ask me to sight read it aloud.

"Have you always mixed up your letters? You really struggle with B and D," she said, without a hint of ridicule. I must have squirmed with embarrassment, but was grateful she hadn't said this in front of the class. "The more you read, the more you'll just recognise the words and then the Bs and Ds won't be such a problem."

So every Thursday and most Tuesday lunch-times I'd read *The Guardian* for Miss Roberts. I was happy to give up my break-time; it offered respite from the bullying on the school yard... and because there were articles about homosexuals – about how their lives might change after the decriminalisation of homosexuality earlier that year. I learned a lot of new words, which I duly noted in my blue vocabulary book; I learned, too, that being a homosexual would leave me open to blackmail, perhaps lead me to alcoholism, I'd almost always be made fun of and shunned by society and I would always be seen as a threat to young boys; a life at the edge.

"Your reading has come on really well," Miss Roberts said at the end of that first year in secondary school.

My understanding of myself had 'come on' too: Being a homosexual meant I'd be someone who could only ever bring disgrace upon my family and scandal upon myself. And so I learned to close doors in my head – or wherever that scary, sordid sense of myself lurked.

I worked at being a good student; perhaps the praise from my teachers – and from Terry and Megan – could temper the wretchedness that I knew was there, somewhere. I quickly realized, however, that I wasn't an all-round scholar. French made no sense at all, but then what little grammar we'd learned in primary school seemed insufficient for all the language rules Mr Green wanted us to learn by heart. After gaining just 18% in the end of year exam it was *au revoir Monsieur Vert*. Physics was fascinating, but I didn't like Mr Cartwright – his rages frightened me, and fear didn't inspire me to learn. And mathematics? Well, I could have done better, but the new maths teacher, Mr Newing distracted me. I suppose he was my first big crush; I failed maths A-level – my first lesson in why mixing business with pleasure is folly. For Mrs Edwards, our biology teacher, I studied late into the night; when others from my class listened to Radio Luxemburg under their bed covers, I read *Plant and Animal Biology* by Vines and Rees. I wanted to do well, as much for her as for myself: At A-level I got an A in biology, and a distinction in an additional scholarship paper that won me £50 for college books.

By the third year of secondary school Miss Enid Jones was teaching us English. She demanded an essay every week and I discovered creative writing, a gift which she encouraged and nurtured... but my spelling was poor and I didn't read 'literature', so I basked in her praise – and shrugged at her praise. Mr Brooks taught us history until the end of the third year; he brought history alive and made it seem relevant to the lives we were living as the nineteen seventies dawned... but he left and Mr Jones took us up to the O-level exams. Walter Jones was killing history for me with sheaves of notes, the single-spaced type blurry from the overused Banda machine in the school office. Mr Brooks had seen Tony through to O-level, and Tony's history notebooks displaced Mr Jones's tome of blotchy paper. No one was more surprised than me when I achieved the highest grade in O-level history at Ysgol Ardudwy in the summer of 1972. But history A-Level with Walter Jones? No way.

However hard I worked, the locks on those closed doors in my mind would sometimes open. One of the older boys, who sometimes used the showers at the same time as my class, came to sit next to me in the school canteen. I remembered that we'd caught one another's eye in the shower and had both immediately looked away. I don't recall now how the flirting proceeded... I think we both just knew! We met in the old barn behind the football pitch; my first homosexual experience with another boy. I was thirteen. It was a thrill and far greater pleasure than self-abuse. We held one another for a long time and even if part of me felt terrified that we'd be discovered I felt strangely safe and comfortable with him.

For days I felt guilty – just like Mr A G Elliot, the man

who wrote *Approaching Manhood* had said I would... but I also held on to the gentleness and pleasure of those minutes in the barn. We met there just once again... and then I saw him necking with a girl in the shelter by the cinema and I didn't seem to exist for him after that. I'd have to find gentleness and pleasure elsewhere.

And I did find it... especially in the summer months when the holiday-makers thronged into Barmouth. Often in a tent or a caravan, occasionally in a squalid lavatory stall in the public toilets at the end of the promenade. And Mr Elliot was right every time; the guilt was crippling.

And then, a much older boy – a man really – hurt me and childhood was over.

As I write this memoir, in the age of internet searches, I do a little investigation into the book Terry so well-meaningly gave my brother Tony and me: *Approaching Manhood – Healthy Sex for Boys* by Andrew George Elliot (writing as Rennie Macandrew), first published by Elliot Right Way Books in 1939. Elliot wrote many 'factual' books about sex at a time when such practical guides were almost unobtainable – which is commendable. In the 1940s and '50s, reliable, sensible information about even the simplest sexual matters was almost never provided, particularly for teenagers and his books were full of 'good sense, good advice, and wisdom' – though they reflected the values and attitudes of an earlier age. Terry gave us the book, I'm certain, with the best of intentions – but the nineteen sixties were a different time, and more enlightened views on sex and sexuality were beginning to be acknowledged and accepted.

4

Tŷ Gwyn

We'd been in Germany almost a year when the time came that Ernst-Peter could no longer walk with us and the dogs. Perhaps it was creeping up for many weeks, but Jutta, not wanting to concede, said nothing about the sleepless nights, or Ernst-Peter's outbursts of anger and aggression at characters on the television, or his many accidents when he could no longer find the toilet. And one day, after too many nights without sleep, she could cope no longer. His circadian rhythms had syncopated... or just died away: night and day no longer having significance. Perhaps he'd sleep for an hour or three on the sofa, but then he'd wander about the house – dressing and undressing, putting on many pairs of trousers... and sweaters... and Jutta's skirts, and throwing the contents of wardrobes to the floor – for hours and hours... and hours and hours... emptying drawers, sweeping the potted plants off the windowsills with a swipe of his arm – trying to climb out of the window so that he could go and find home. The swamp that is German bureaucracy is daunting but efficient. Jupp waded through the on-line forms, the phone calls, the interviews and the sheer exhausting anxiety of it all and incredibly, within twenty-four hours had found a place for him in a residential home. So all our lives and routines were changed. The care home was immaculate. We visited him two or three times a week... and were met with a blank gaze. And then, one Tuesday afternoon, his wife and two sons at his side, Ernst-Peter died without much palaver.

"There's always a lot of talk in small villages," the priest says. Jutta sits with her sister and Jupp in our dining room to arrange the funeral. "I'd be grateful if we can be candid around this table," the priest continues, and sips hot tea from one of my mother-in-law's best Meissen china cups – which she'd had us bring over from her house because our mugs were not suitable for Herr Pastor Wieners. He eyes everyone as I bring the coffee through from the kitchen. "I don't want to eulogise Ernst-Peter only to have someone come to me later and ask why I hadn't done my homework." I wondered what he already knew about my father-in-law... and whether any more scandals would be revealed.

My own father, Terry, died in July 2001. He'd developed prostate cancer during the last decades of the century, but had been too embarrassed to tell his doctor that he leaked and sometimes even pissed himself. When he complained of pain across his shoulders my mother made him go to see the GP, by which time there were secondary cancers in his bones – and then in his liver. His death wasn't easy, quick or pleasant.

At his funeral, my dad's brother, Uncle Neil, told Tony, Jupp and me about how he and Terry had a big falling-out over family secrets.

"Now that the old bugger's dead you'd better know the story," he said.

Stand on the quayside with your back to the Mawddach's broad mouth and before you the Davy Jones' Locker spills its bustle onto the wide pavement; it's been a café for as long as I can remember. In 1565, when Elizabeth I instituted a survey of the havens and creeks of Wales in an effort to suppress piracy, this building, Tŷ Gwyn, was one of only four buildings recorded in *Abermowe*. Architecturally, it's a 'first floor hall house', built by Gruffudd Fychan of Cors y Gedol Hall, Dyffryn, in 1460. It's acknowledged as the oldest building in Barmouth. In Victorian times it was converted from a boat shed and store to a multiple-occupancy dwelling. Imagine, if you can, a small window in the gable – that small triangle of wall between the edges of the sloping roof. Behind that window, in a Dickensian hovel, my grandfather spent the early years of his life in some squalor.

Mary Jones, my great-grandmother, lived in the roof space apartment at Tŷ Gwyn with her own children, her mother, Rebecca (and Rebecca's sometimes 'husband' Charles who was not the girls' father), her older sister, Ann, and Ann's three 'bastard' children. Until 1976 my grandfather's half-brother and half-sister, great auntie Anne (not to be confused with her own aunt who was called Ann – mentioned above) and great uncle Will, lived in that same roof space. Every Saturday, as a boy, I took them cakes and tarts made by my grandmother, and did their errands; Auntie Anne was badly disabled – her right foot sticking out at an angle that made you wince – so she never strayed much beyond the foot of their outside stairs. In the autumn and winter, when there weren't many tourists about, I'd fetch the tobacco for Auntie Anne's clay pipe from the little shop next to the Last Inn – Mrs Williams behind the counter always had a tin of Golden Virginia in a white paper bag waiting for me. During the holiday season Auntie Anne wouldn't buy tobacco; she'd send me out onto the quayside to collect cigarette butts in a child's sand bucket and through the week she'd winkle out the tobacco from each fag end until she had enough to fill her pipe. Uncle Will never said much – I don't remember him ever speaking to me; he always wore a blue sailor's sweater with holes in the elbows – and his cheeks were red-veined. Their home in the roof space smelled of cats' piss and a big ginger Tom always slept on a cushion in the hearth.

"All the children were born in the workhouse." Neil continued.

My grandfather, Samuel Jones, was born in January 1901 in the Union Workhouse in Dolgellau. The workhouse minute book records an entry in respect of Mary Jones of Tŷ Gwyn, Barmouth, and her son Samuel, authorizing the Clerk of the Guardians to enforce an Order in Bastardy upon Enoch Egerton, a tailor from Bridge Street in Corris. Mr Egerton must duly have acknowledged paternity – or at the very least intimate congress with Mary – as the confinement fee was noted as 'paid in full'. Mary had two other 'bastard' children before Samuel was born, William – in 1888, and Anne – in 1897, and then a fourth child, Edmund, born in 1907.

"The minute book of the Elder's meetings at Caersalem, the Welsh Calvinistic Methodist chapel, had an entry from the late 1890's... both the sisters were excommunicated on the same day," Neil said. "I saw it with my own eyes – in beautiful copperplate writing – but like a fool, I forgot to write down the date."

As children, Samuel and William never knew one another. A year before Samuel was born, the Barmouth magistrates deemed Mary Jones to be a negligent mother and William – a 'naughty boy' about town, but not delinquent – was sent to the Industrial Training Ship *Clio*, moored in the Menai Strait, to be educated and trained for a role as a seaman in the Royal Navy. William grew into a short man – too short for the Royal Navy, and from the *Clio* he entered the Mercantile Marine only returning to Barmouth in 1922 to become a ferryboat man on the Mawddach, his motor launch, *Pansy*, one of the first motorboats on the river.

In the first years of the twentieth century, Samuel lived in the crowded roof space at Tŷ Gwyn. His half-sister, Anne, who had a badly broken leg that was never properly set, spent much of this time in her grandmother's bed, but Samuel had his cousins, Gwen and Evan, for company. In later years, Samuel always referred to Gwen and Evan as his sister and brother, so intertwined was their early life together. But Samuel's childhood came to an abrupt end when his mother sold him into agricultural labour at Glanymorfa, a farm on the banks of the Dysynni River near Tywyn, some miles south of Barmouth.

"Dad did talk about it, just once," Neil said. "He couldn't remember exactly how old he was but he thought it was the late summer before his ninth birthday... in the hiring fair, when farmers from around the area hired local people for a few days or weeks to bring in the harvest. He did remember being in the farmer's cart and calling out to his mother as she walked away – he remembered that she didn't turn back to wave him goodbye."

At Glanymorfa, Samuel slept on a hay filled mattress in one of the sheds. Ginny, the only child of the farm and perhaps three or four years older, did show him some kindness, bringing him an extra blanket after he'd complained that he was cold at night... and sometimes a bowl of cold rice pudding left over after Sunday dinner. He worked seven days a week – a boy doing a man's work. He was often hungry and cold in his years on the farm, but then the Great War came. In January 1915, just days after his fourteenth birthday, which nobody acknowledged, he walked away from Glanymorfa and as a goods train slowed through the halt at Tonfanau he climbed into one of the open goods trucks and hitched a ride. Years of manual labour had turned the boy into a strong young man; at fourteen he passed easily for a sixteen-year-old and he found work at the Birmingham Small Arms Company in Sparkbrook, producing rifles, Lewis guns, shells, motorcycles and other vehicles for the war effort.

"The landlady at his digs was kind to him," Neil said. "He liked her, and because she seemed to have a soft spot for him she did his laundry at no extra charge."

The war with Germany wasn't over by Christmas. During 1915, legislation was drafted to introduce conscription and in January 1916 the Military Service Act was passed. Imposed on all single men aged between 18 and 41, the draft was unpopular. Working in the manufacture of war goods, Samuel didn't give the possibility of being called up much thought, but just after his sixteenth birthday, in January 1917 – having added two years to his age to get the job at the factory – Samuel received his draft papers and he joined the Royal Welsh Fusiliers.

In the last weeks of his initial training, Samuel contracted double pneumonia and found himself in a military hospital when his unit was sent to France. The rebellion in Ireland gained momentum during 1917 and in November, recovered from his illness, he was sent to Ireland where he remained until 1921.

Samuel began an ex-serviceman's apprenticeship as a cabinet maker in Newtown (then in Montgomeryshire) after his demobilisation. During his time in Ireland, along with his taste for stout, he'd become a keen and skilled snooker player and he quickly made new friends around the pubs in the town. He got on particularly well with the Baxter brothers... and was sweet on their sister, Gladys. John Samuel Baxter, a hero of the campaign in Galipoli, wanted better for 'his Glad', his only daughter, and Samuel's evasiveness about his family only fuelled Mr Baxter's doubts about their courtship. Unbeknown to the lovesick couple, John Baxter took the train to Barmouth, and over a pint of the Last Inn's best bitter he learned about the impropriety of the family that lived in the roof space at Tŷ Gwyn, the publican even referring to Samuel's mother and her sister as 'trollops' and 'baggage'.

Samuel and Gladys eloped and married in secret in 1926. John Baxter had done his best to stop his daughter marrying the 'illegitimate son of a whore' – but Glad knew her own mind. They were married for fifty-five years and had four sons; my father, Terry, was their second son.

"If I'm honest," Uncle Neil said, "I should have been more sensitive to why Terry didn't want to know about the Tŷ Gwyn tribe. Because of his gammy leg he never left Barmouth – no National Service, not enough money to send him to college. Barmouth was his life; Megan and you two boys, the silver band, the Buffs, playing his banjo in the jazz group... and he was close to his Mam, because he was so disabled, I suppose – she'd probably spoiled him a bit. Our Mam, knowing some of Samuel's history, never put a foot wrong – being respectable and accepted was what she worked for every day of her married life, and I think Terry believed that dredging up that history, and him knowing about Dad's family, would hurt her."

Tony and I were fascinated... and amazed that we could have reached our late forties and not known what had gone on in the roof space at Tŷ Gwyn.

"I wonder, if I'd known this story when I was growing up, whether I'd have felt quite so much shame and guilt about being gay," I said to Jupp as we drove home from the funeral. "That fear I had of bringing disgrace on the family was what made me so secretive – living that double life for so long."

5

WDR4 – Thunder in my Heart

Being so close to the edge, the only German radio station we can pick up clearly on the bedside alarm clock – standing tall like a dyke amid a flood of Dutch – is WDR4...Westdeutscher Rundfunk... twenty-four hours of 'oldies' and chat. In amongst the German and French songs there's a lot of popular music in English from the nineteen-forties onward. Listening to WDR4 doesn't help my German too much, but the memories these songs from my past unlock are often wonderful to savour in those half-awake minutes... and sometimes poignant.

Leo Sayer is singing *Thunder in my Heart*... and I remember Dafydd Owen. He messed me around, but then, in Aberystwyth, in 1977, I was in no shape to be exploring such a liaison; having turned 21, it was my first lawful gay sexual relationship, but infused with doubts and memories of electric shock aversion therapy, it went badly wrong. I probably messed him around too... but we stayed friends. Meck re-worked Sayer's seventies performance and released *Thunder in my Heart Again* in

2006 when it topped the charts in the UK in February; Jupp and I were planning our Civil Partnership.

I was one of the founding members of the Lesbian-Gay-Bisexual (LGB) Forum Cymru, a sister organisation to Stonewall, the London-based LGB equality charity. This forum, founded in the first months of 2001, was the result of several trends. The National Assembly for Wales had established an equal opportunities committee, chaired by Edwina Hart, the minister for finance, local government and communities. It had also established an equality policy unit within the Promoting Equality in Wales Project Development Fund. At the same time, Stonewall's executive director, Angela Mason, had been lobbying the national assembly to seek out the 'authentic' voice of LGB communities across Wales, and she'd talked with LGB groups across the county during the autumn of 2000 about how they might network and become a credible, representative voice to which the assembly could listen.

As the Forum's first co-chair with Gloria Jenkins from Cardiff, I became a member of Stonewall's Board of Trustees and served for a couple of years. The fight for equal marriage rights was amongst Stonewall's campaigns, and whilst I had no direct involvement in that particular struggle, most of our close circle assumed, because of this association, that we'd be 'married' – or 'civilised' some would joke (because ultimately the legal status between same-sex couples became known as a Civil Partnership) as soon as the law was finally pushed through... after all, we'd been together for twenty years. In all of that time together, Jupp and I had never discussed 'getting married', but shortly after the legislation became law in 2005 he proposed; we were in Rome on a short break, and during a candle-lit supper in a cosy restaurant looking out onto the Tiber he went down onto one knee. The waiters applauded, wished us well, and didn't charge us for the wine or the dessert!

Our initial thought was to go quietly to the Registry Office with two witnesses – but on a dull, but warm and dry day in April 2006, more than a hundred people, family and friends from every chapter of our lives, came to celebrate with us in Portmeirion. The ceremony, in Welsh, German and English was something we both worked on for some weeks, and for many of our guests, it was a memorable first Civil Partnership. A long-time friend from Aberystwyth, Ann Williams, played the harp – some traditional Welsh and German melodies – and Philip Roderick, a friend from student days and one of six clergy celebrating with us, played his Hang drum. We were both moved very deeply by the warmth and sincerity of the joy expressed by those who gathered to be with us. For me, the evidence of their love and acceptance on that day healed so many of the wounds inflicted by decades of scorn and rejection.

Jupp's father, Ernst-Peter, chose not to come to Wales

to celebrate with us. He wouldn't talk with us about it. He'd told Jutta to tell us that someone had to stay in Effeld to look after the dog. And Dafydd Owen, who'd remained a friend for thirty years, was absent too; cancer had claimed him just weeks before.

6

Electricity

We'd been in Germany just three months when I almost fell from the top of a three metre ladder whilst painting the ceiling of the stair well in the house we were slowly turning into a home. I've never suffered from vertigo – I've jumped between Adam and Eve on the summit of Tryfan more times than I can remember and always been the one to suggest we climb the tower, take the cliff path, ride the chair lift or hike to the highest peak. The bottom of the ladder was jammed against the riser on the fourth step of the staircase and couldn't go anywhere, but everything around me moved. I managed to get down the ladder, light-headed and out of breath, and sitting on the bottom step waiting to 'come around', I got the sense that there was a basket of writhing snakes in my chest – but no ache... no pain. Then, in just a few moments, the snakes settled, my breathing steadied and the wooziness was gone. And I remembered that it had happened once before, in less dramatic circumstances – throwing sticks for the dogs into the waves on Barmouth beach on one of the last days before our move; I'd sat on the sand then, until the weirdness passed... Nel barking for her stick and Wash, his head cocked, looking inquisitive. On my feet again, walking the beach, I thought I'd probably done too much upping and downing, too quickly picking up the sticks and throwing them whenever the dogs brought them back to me.

I have coronary heart disease. Not long after my forty-seventh birthday, in July 2003, after three weeks of miserable, on-and-off 'indigestion', I was admitted into our local general hospital where the diagnosis was confirmed – an acute narrowing in a branch of the main cardiac artery that feeds the left ventricle; it's called the LAD – the Left Anterior Descending. Such a blockage is also called 'the widow-maker'. Transferred in a blue light ambulance to the Liverpool Heart and Chest Hospital, I had a stent fitted into the LAD. Had the artery become completely blocked or burst during the procedure I would have needed immediate open heart surgery to perform a by-pass... or Jupp might have become a widower and they'd have to think about changing the moniker.

Physically, I recovered quickly, but my self-confidence and my sense of self were badly shaken and even ten weeks of cardiac rehabilitation didn't entirely restore my poise. I learnt to make some lifestyle changes; stairs, never escalators and lifts, less red meat, less food in general – though I'd hovered just above the top end of my ideal weight range I'd never been seriously overweight, but the cardiologist's advice was to aim for the lower end of that range and lose just a couple of stones. But I looked so gaunt at 11 stone so settled for twelve. I needed to drink less alcohol too, and take more regular exercise – hence the dogs! This may sound odd, but I also learned to 'listen' to my heart – becoming aware of its rhythms, and whether there was any heartache, as in angina. I've been on medication ever since... beta-blockers, statins, ACE inhibitors, and aspirin. I found being drug dependent, so young, a burden... I still find it so; it doesn't fit with my self-perception.

Because of my medical history, I saw a cardiologist within days of almost falling from the ladder. Jupp had to come with me as my German was still scant – which wasn't easy for him being a squeamish type. *Herr Doktor* Brück was thorough, but distant in his 'bedside-manner': I felt that I was being processed according to the protocol laid out in the sheaf of forms he had on his clip board... perhaps if I'd had more language we may have chatted and my impression of him may then have been different. A 24 hour ECG – electrocardiography is the process of recording the electrical activity of the heart over a period of time using electrodes placed over the skin – revealed some disturbances in my heart's rhythm, a mild form of atrial fibrillation, where one chamber of the heart beats too quickly and throws the heart's rhythm into chaos; so that's the basket of writhing snakes! Dr Brück upped the dose of my beta-blocker, "...that usually controls erratic rhythms," he said, and prescribed an anticoagulant because blood clots within the heart are a common consequence of arrhythmia because the chambers don't properly empty with each beat.

Having electrodes attached to my body triggered some dark memories that I chose to block... a new country... a new life – there was no need to re-visit that territory. I busied myself again with house decorating, but dizziness became a fairly frequent companion. By September the snakes in my chest were writhed more frequently, so the dose of beta-blocker was raised again – but by the beginning of November my irregular pulse had 'stabilized' at between 150 and 160 beats per minute and the snakes didn't seem to rest. Both my family doctor and Dr Brück were of the opinion that I should go into the hospital, where they would first try to shock my heart into a normal rhythm, and if that failed, a surgical procedure called ablation would be necessary.

Cardioversion is a routine procedure. Sticky pads were attached to my chest and back. The technician, a fair, forty-something with tattooed arms and a smile that revealed a golden tooth, was careful to explain what he was doing, his English better than my German. The defibrillator machine would shock my heart when he applied the electrodes to the pads on my chest, jolting it back into its normal rhythm... "But we might have to do it more than once. All these machines measure and regulate..." he waved his hand at the array of screens as his English failed him. "I'll give you a shot of this," he said, holding up the syringe. "You'll only be asleep for about ten minutes and when you wake up I hope your heart will be calm."

A hospital in another time, in another country. A consulting room at the north Wales Hospital, Denbigh, on a snowy January day in 1975, Dr Dafydd Alun Jones, consultant psychiatrist, explaining the electric shock treatment. I didn't want to be a homosexual. I didn't want to be bullied and ridiculed for the rest of my life. I was eighteen years old and crippled by the shame of it, and the disgrace it brought upon my family. I was eighteen years old and paralysed by the guilt of my clandestine, sexually promiscuous exploration of other men. I was eighteen years old and I was contemplating suicide. I was eighteen years old and could make my own decisions about medical treatment – and the treatment on offer was Electric Shock Aversion Therapy. Many years later I discovered that this form of 'cure' for homosexuality, still considered an illness as late as the 1980s, had been largely discredited by the late 1960s in all the journals of psychiatry in Europe and the United States. Dr Jones clearly hadn't kept himself informed, and whilst I'm gracious enough to trust that he was doing what he believed was clinically apposite, I can't forgive his professional indolence.

"I had to shock you twice," the technician with tattoos said in German accented English. "Your heart likes to race." He'd removed the sticky pads from my chest and back by the time I'd regained consciousness and he was busy wiring me up to a portable heart monitor in readiness for my return to the ward.

Within only a couple of hours the snakes in my chest were agitated again and the ward doctor confirmed that I'd need to undergo pulmonary vein isolation (PVI) ablation. Her English was about as bad as my German, but I found some NHS websites that explained the procedure: through a catheter inserted via an artery in my groin the doctors could access the inside of my heart and locate the areas of muscle that were generating the erratic electrical impulses causing the arrhythmia. Once isolated, these areas of muscle inside my heart would be destroyed – either by burning them or freezing them – and the scar tissue formed as a result of the burn would block any errant signals that may still occur.

Later in the day the cardiologist who was to perform the procedure came to speak with me. She looked as if she'd come straight into work from a gallop on horseback, the coloured streaks in her hair all confused, her face weather-worn... cheeks dimpled and rosy. Her voice was deep and cracked, as if she smoked forty a day – but she's a heart surgeon, so perhaps not. She had an 'I've-lived-a-life' look and a smile that made you want to believe in her. So I did believe her when she told me, in fluent English, "We are a specialist centre for cardiac catheterisation, and although ablation sounds quite frightening, we do it routinely here – it's quite safe and successful the first time in most patients."

Before the ablation could be carried out my heart had to be scanned, to be sure there were no blood clots lurking; when the heart beats irregularly and erratically there is always a danger that the chambers don't properly empty – and that's when clots form. But a racing heart can't be scanned, so I paid another visit to the man with the golden tooth who shocked my heart into normal rhythm just long enough for the scanner to do its job.

In the old Victorian asylum in Denbigh I was shocked if my body responded to erotic images of men. A sheath was supposed to have been placed over my penis that could measure tumescence, and electric shocks would be delivered through electrodes in a wrist band. Perhaps because the treatment was outmoded, or because so few men had sought a cure for homosexuality at the north Wales Hospital, no sheath, called a penis transponder, could be found.

I was naked from the waist down. I was shown

homosexual pornography, the like of which I'd never seen, and if my penis so much as twitched, began to swell or became erect, I was shocked. For between thirty minutes and an hour, every day for many weeks my sexual response to erotic images of men became fused with electric shocks that jolted unpleasantness through my body. I'm not sure when I began to realize that Dr Dafydd Alun Jones' prescribed treatment was abusive.

The ablation procedure took *Frau Doktor* and her junior assistant almost four hours – electrically generated heat sources torching the centres of specious impulses that had accelerated my heartbeat to a chaotic arrhythmia. And my heart was tamed.

Once I lost faith in the aversion therapy I lost the will to continue with it... and once I'd begun to see the electric shocks as an abuse, I lost my faith in Dafydd Alun Jones. But I also felt trapped, my thinking dulled by tranquilizers and anti-depressant drugs, and by some boundary of my own creation that made the rejection of the help I was being offered an impossible option. So the pornography and electric orgasms continued.

7

WDR4 – Puppy Love

Waking up to Donny Osmond singing *Puppy Love* takes me back to a small tent on Fegla Fawr – the day my childhood ended, if not my innocence.

Just after I'd finished my O-levels, in the summer of 1972, I cycled in the light evenings after finishing my holiday job in the chip shop. Crossing Barmouth Bridge, I recognized someone I'd seen hanging around the public toilets at the end of the promenade. He was older, maybe nineteen or twenty. I smiled at him as I approached and he grinned and said, "Hello, I know you, don't I?"

"From the end of the prom," I said, half a question, half a statement.

"I think so," he said, laughing.

"You on holiday then?" I said.

"Yes… I'm camping on that hill at the end of the bridge," he said, pointing into the near distance. "A tent is a bit more comfortable than in the lav… but only if you want to."

I wanted to – and I was relieved that I'd bathed after work and didn't smell of fried fish and vinegar. I pushed my bike as we walked together across the bridge. I recall that we seemed easy with one another.

It had been a sunny day and it was stifling inside the small tent.

"I'll turn the radio on," he said. "We don't want anyone to hear us."

I'd never been completely naked with another boy and I liked lying next to him, touching him, him touching me. We lay like that for what seemed like a long time, just touching... and kissing. I'd never kissed like that before. I liked how he tasted and I liked the way he ran his tongue along my lip. But then he spread my legs and started to push into me.

"I don't want to do that," I said.

Donny Osmond started to sing about his puppy love.

"I won't hurt you, honest," he said, caressing me gently. "I won't hurt you.... If you just relax... it'll feel really nice."

He moved back beside me and caressed and kissed me some more... then he licked his finger, "Just relax," he said, and stroked gently between my legs. It felt nice... I'd never touched myself there – and I was grateful again that I'd had a bath.

But then he was between my legs again, pushing.

"I don't want to," I said again – but he'd pushed hard into me. And Donny wailed:

Someone, help me, help me, help me please;

Is the answer up above?
How can I, oh how can I tell them?
This is not a puppy love.

I had to push my bike back over the bridge to Barmouth.

8

WDR4 – San Francisco

Another morning on the edge. The new Interior Minister in the Berlin government, Horst Seehofer, proclaims that Islam doesn't belong in Germany. Jupp says Seehofer has his eye on the elections in Bavaria, his home state, where the AfD – the far-right *Alternative für Deutschland* – have gained strength and pose a real threat to his party, the Christian Social Union (the sister party in Bavaria to Angela Merkel's less conservative Christian Democratic Union).

"He's got to convince his electorate that he's tough on Merkel's refugee policy or he may lose out to the AfD," Jupp says.

"But haven't there been Turkish *Gastarbeiter* here since the 1960s?"

"There's not far off three million Turkish people here," Jupp says, "and I suppose most of them are Muslims."

"Imagine if he'd said that Judaism doesn't belong in Germany," I offer, not believing Seehofer can be a credible politician. "Do you think he really can't see the analogy?"

"He probably believes what he's saying and thinks it's what a majority of Bavarians want to hear."

The news comes to an end and Scott McKenzie is San Francisco bound with flowers in his hair.

I was twenty-five when I arrived in the San Francisco Bay Area to take up a World Council of Churches scholarship at Berkeley's Graduate Theological Union (GTU). The bursary, from Pacific School of Religion (PSR), had been granted for one year, tuition and living expenses, to investigate and reflect theologically upon lesbian and gay experience of church, and how the different churches in that part of northern California – already a 'gay mecca' – were responding to lesbians and gay men.

My understanding of myself as a gay man had matured. I'd met many gay men who were 'out and proud' and who lived happy, useful, creative lives. Through the fledgling Gay Christian Movement (much later to become the Lesbian and Gay Christian Movement), I came to understand how homosexuality and Christianity could be reconciled – and I had come to accept that I was made in God's image; an identity which carried a responsibility (the fine print of which I was still trying to de-cypher). The reverend Jim Cotter, one of the founding members of that movement, became a life-long friend until his death in 2014, and for his wisdom I will always be grateful. But in much of my every-day life I was still closeted – afraid, even, that certain people would 'find out' and reject me... and sexually, I was damaged. Dr D A Jones's electric shock aversion therapy hadn't *cured* my *deviance* and made me *normal*, but it had very successfully skewed my responses to sexual desire, and in sexual situations I experienced flash-backs to those shocking episodes of the first months of 1975. I'd had fleeting dalliances, even a year-long relationship with Bob Harney, a lecturer at Aberystwyth University, but my sexual ambivalence hindered my sex life and I believed it would doom my chances of finding a partner. Even masturbation – I'd consciously stopped thinking of it as self-abuse – was sullied by the memory of shocks; celibacy, the focus of much of my prayer life, was an option I'd been considering seriously for two or three years. I suppose, then, that the man who arrived in California in late August 1981 was on the brink of committing to asceticism – perhaps even a life in religious community, and certainly not about to wear flowers in his cropped hair and go in search of free love.

Orientation Week at Pacific School of Religion (PSR) – the ecumenical seminary at which I was enrolled – broke ice and helped the in-coming class of mostly 'mature students', people from across the United States and from around the world, to settle, to integrate, and gain some insight into Berkeley life – because didn't Berkeley have a world-wide reputation as a hot-bed of protest and wackiness? It also did much to de-mystify the alphabet soup of acronyms on Berkeley's Holy Hill where all the

Graduate Theological Union's seminaries were known by their initials... CDSP (the Church Divinity School of the Pacific – Anglican), PLTS (the Pacific Lutheran Theological Seminary), ABSW (the American Baptist Seminary of the West), JSTB (the Jesuit School of Theology at Berkeley) – and many more! Classes in all of the GTU seminaries were open to any student enrolled in a member seminary and the theological education thus on offer spanned the gulf between conservative evangelicism and snake-belly-low. Two mornings during that introductory week were spent helping us incomers understand class registration across the GTU and ensuring denominational requirements for those in the ordination process would be met.

The final afternoon of Orientation Week found us in the seminary chapel for a service of welcome and dedication to the task in hand – study and theological reflection. The Dean of Students, the Reverend Barbara Roche offered some introductory comments, which included a brief demographic of the in-coming class... so many Methodists... black student numbers up by fifty per cent... eight Roman Catholic women denied enrolment in any of the RC seminaries... oldest student 68 – youngest 23... five international students, "...including this year's World Council of Churches Scholar from Wales, John Sam Jones – an openly gay man who has come to learn about ministry with our lesbian and gay brothers and sisters; he's one of the six openly gay students we welcome this fall."

What? She'd just told the world that I'm gay?

By the end of the service the inner turmoil caused by Barbara Roche's public outing of my sexuality had quelled. Whatever her motive, she'd offered me an opportunity to explore a new way to live my life without the need for evasiveness and fear of rejection; the possibility of grasping the door handle of the closet into which I so conveniently retreated when challenging prejudice and misconception was just too frightening to contemplate, and throwing open the door once and for all. Indeed, she was even offering the possibility of finding the keys to those doors still locked in my psyche. Barbara Roche had offered a challenge – that from that moment, John Sam Jones, openly gay man, was destined to be dealt with!

I didn't see her immediately after chapel, but later, in the 'meet-the-faculty' wine and canapé reception, I thanked her.

"Welcome to Berkeley," she said. "Welcome to Pacific School of Religion... if you can't be yourself here then we're failing the Gospel. Go read Irenaeus... 'The glory of God is the fully alive human being', not the woman who believes she has to conceal part of her humanity because patriarchal tradition has mistrusted and misinterpreted God's creation, or the man who's blind to the diversity of God's humanity."

I remember thinking she was a bit earnest, even a bit 'bezerkeley' (the commonly used euphemism for crazy Berkeley folk) but her words brought back something Huw Wynne Griffith, the minister at Seilo in Aberystwyth, had said to me in those dark days after I'd tried to commit suicide. At my bedside in Bronglais hospital he held my hand. He didn't know about the pornography and the electric shock treatment, or how what I had come to understand as Dr D A Jones' abuse had pushed me over the edge, but he knew enough. "The label that society puts on you is not as important as the way you choose to live your life, John," Huw said. "You're not defined by a label. God wants each one of us to be the best person we can be... and if you are a homosexual... if that's a part of who you are, then you've got to ask yourself what it will mean for you to live your life as the best homosexual you can be. That's for you and God to work out together."

Dr Cindy Coleman had served as an ordained minister in the Lutheran Church, but after coming out as a lesbian – and losing both her husband and her 'good standing' in the church – she'd moved west to California and trained as a psychotherapist specialising in sexuality issues. I first met her at a pot-luck supper on campus and we talked briefly over guacamole and corn chips, and then, a few days later, I saw her in the coffee shop on Euclid Avenue and we talked some more. She explained that she had a sliding scale of charges and we came to an understanding. I had no concern that I was 'rushing into something Berkeley-wacky'; I had one year in California ahead of me – one chance in a new environment to slough off the old skin... though I knew well enough that my problems were more than skin deep! The faculty and students I'd spoken with knew of Cindy Coleman's reputation and had praised her work... and I'd secured a job in the seminary kitchen that would augment my bursary and I could therefore afford to pay her. I wanted to live out of the shadows.

I met with Cindy every week for a fifty-minute-hour through that first year in California – a year during which I also wrestled with my sense of calling to ministry. After deciding to enrol in the master's programme in pastoral theology and self-fund a further two years at PSR, I continued to see her for much of the second year. 'Unlearning', is how she described some of our process; unlearning the assumptions I'd drawn from my parents' silence about sex... unlearning the guilt and shame which the author of *Approaching Manhood* and *Guardian* journalists had convinced me I would experience... unlearning the sense of inadequacy that years of being bullied had fostered... unlearning that being homosexual made me sordid, sinful and corrupt. We spent some months exploring the theme of forgiveness; forgiving a psychiatrist with his trigger-happy finger on the switch of a shock box... forgiving a rapist... forgiving myself for attempting self-murder. And we tried on many different pairs of tinted spectacles – because how we see the world around us stimulates the response we make to that world: Cindy had me think about this for many weeks – that the tint in the glasses can help us see the subtleties of a situation, and thus help us mould a response that is often different from the one we might make at first glance through plain glass.

Because of her own theological training, Cindy recommended books she believed would support my growth. Among the many titles she suggested, three dog-eared volumes remain on my book shelf to this day – *The Wounded Healer* by Henri Nouwen, *Suffering* by Dorothee Sölle and *Man's Search for Meaning* by Viktor Frankl. At the risk of being over-simplistic, Nouwen helped me to understand how even the deepest wounds can be transformed into reserves of compassion. Sölle convinced me that in our lives 'shit just happens' – I'm paraphrasing – and when difficult life events throw us off balance we do have some choice in how we respond; in that sense we chose the way we suffer our misfortunes – some with a cup half empty, some with a cup half full. And Frankl? He perhaps spoke loudest to me in those post-suicide days, helping me on the continuing journey to live every day in search of the meaning of my life – as a Welsh man... as a gay man... as a Christian... as an exile... and strive to be the best that I can be.

Throughout my time in Berkeley I carried a full class load in each semester and took further classes in the winter and summer breaks – so for three years I was in class for fifty weeks a year. It was a heavy academic burden, but I had no need to prove to myself that I was an A-student, though I did have to demonstrate some degree of academic excellence. As there was always an option to take a class on a pass/fail basis, I'd choose, at the beginning of each term, just one of the courses for a grade – usually a 'core' subject like Systematic Theology, Church History, and New Testament. My transcript on graduation with a master's degree in divinity in the summer of 1984 showed that I'd achieved just one A grade per academic session in a sea of passes.

The kitchen work, mostly dish-washing and cleaning in the first year, but then a promotion to breakfast cook in the second year, didn't bring in enough income to cover my expenses once my scholarship had come to an end. My brother Tony, by then an orthopaedic surgeon in Liverpool, was generous in his support, as were my parents, Terry and Megan – but I was always uncomfortable asking them for money. Indeed, there were occasions when the whole California adventure looked like it would fold because of a lack of funds. But twice, anonymous benefactors came to my aid. My third-year tuition fees were paid (I found out later) by Joe Santoyo – a banker, and Richard Bates – an ordained minister in his life before he came out, a gay couple from Bethany United Methodist Church in San Francisco – the church where I served as a half-time assistant minister to fulfil my Field Education requirements. It would be more than thirty years before Audrey Ward, one of my seminary class-mates, disclosed that she and her husband Bob, had paid my second year tuition fees. I found such generosity humbling... but at the time I also acknowledged it to be a sign that my journey was being validated.

Just after Christmas in 1982, during my second year at seminary, I fell in love with Michael Wyatt. He was a third-year student at the Episcopal seminary – the Church Divinity School of the Pacific. Already an ordained deacon, and on his way to being priested, he also fell in love with me. There were no flash-backs to the shocking time in the Denbigh asylum... no trace of shame, anguish or guilt. I was twenty-six, and for the first time I knew the sweetness of romantic love and learned the joy of sexual intimacy. I enjoyed sex – a lot... and celibacy, such a high calling, was no longer an option. Michael wrote poems for me, and put one of my favourite Dylan Thomas poems to music – he was a gifted pianist, organist and composer. He was cultured; well-read, a linguist – having lived in Europe and South America, a lover of theatre: A renaissance man, I suppose... and at twenty-nine, he was also an alcoholic. In the eighteen months we were together I never saw him drunk. We never argued. We laughed a lot. We never disappointed one another. We knew our time together would be short and we lived it to its sacred fullness.

My parents flew out to attend my graduation. I was happy that they'd decided to come; in ten days they'd get some sense of my life in California and perhaps I might come to know them a little better. We did a lot of sight-seeing, but then, northern California has so much to offer the tourist and San Francisco is a beautiful city; around most corners, and without much effort, there's something to see that can fascinate, bring a smile, even take the breath away. We drank cocktails at the *Top of the Mark*... we sailed across the bay to Alcatraz... we walked across the Golden Gate Bridge... we even wandered amongst the giant Sequoias in Muir Woods. But the sight of men holding hands on Castro Street disturbed them, and when I told them that there'd be an afternoon when they'd have to fend for themselves because I needed to visit the young men I'd befriended on the AIDS ward at San Francisco General Hospital– Terry started to lecture me about the gay plague and how it was spread by sick men behaving like animals. "That's what happens to men 'like that,'" he said.

"Men like me, you mean?" I said, as gently and as non-threateningly as I could.

"So Dafydd Alun Jones didn't cure you then," he said, disappointment in his voice.

"Don't start on this, Terry," Megan said.

I didn't respond. I'd grown so much in my understanding of myself... and I'd grown so far from their understanding of who their son was... and who their son had become. And I remembered with gratitude that Terry had declined Jones' request to sign the papers that would have placed me on a "section" in the old asylum in Denbigh... 'Whatever else he is' he'd told Dr Jones, 'my son isn't mad.'

9

One Bread, One Body

Effeld's Roman Catholic priest, *Herr Pastor* Thomas Wieners, won't offer me communion. He arrived early to discuss the arrangements for Ernst-Peter's funeral and whilst we waited for Jupp and his mother to come over from her sister's house, we talked over a cup of tea. I told him some of my history; how much of my theological education in Berkeley had been with the Dominicans, the Jesuits and the Franciscans – but was careful not to mention Rosemary Radford Ruether or Hans Küng, both of whom had given the Vatican cause for concern. Thomas Wieners speaks better English than I speak German, and he likes to speak English, very precisely, very eloquently – so I didn't misunderstand his unwillingness to invite a non-Roman Catholic to share in the Eucharist.

"If you had chosen not to tell me that you are a Protestant I would have been none the wiser and you could have communicated," he said.

"But if I'd chosen not to tell you, I would have had to carry the burden of deceiving you by omission, and perhaps, eventually, put you in a position where you might feel you'd have to approach me because you'd heard that I am not a Roman Catholic... this is a small village and people talk."

He was quiet for a few moments. Because I don't know him, I didn't have a clue how to interpret his gestures so I was momentarily disconcerted... but then he said, "I'm grateful that you're able to show me such pastoral sensitivity... of course, when you come up to the communion rail I will offer you a blessing."

In the months after I'd been pulled back from suicide I spent a lot of time with Huw and Mair Wynne Griffith in Aberystwyth. Their love and unconditional acceptance of my difference were the anchors that held firm when all I could hope for was that I might get through the next hours of the day. And so the days I 'got through' became weeks, and the weeks I 'got through' became months. Huw would sometimes offer a book he'd been reading – *Is the Homosexual my Neighbour?* by Mollenkott and Scanzoni... Norman Pittenger's *Time for Consent* – and Mair would offer up whole days just to sit beside me; 'the journey is home', she'd say, 'and sometimes, when it's uncomfortable or when we're feeling lost, we need company on that journey'.

She liked to play a cassette of chants that one of her daughters had brought back from Taizé, a monastic community in France that young people from across

Europe and north America had been drawn to for some time because of its inclusive simplicity. I particularly liked *Ubi Caritas, et amor, Deus ibi est* – where charity and love reside, God resides – and I believe that listening to the brothers from Taizé chanting not only calmed my troubled mind but awakened my senses to meditation and prayer. On a visit to Liverpool to stay with my brother Tony, I bought a couple of LPs of Taizé chants from the catholic book shop on Bold Street. I chanted along with the community at Taizé most days during my undergraduate years – and Leah Owen and Delwyn Siôn were part of the sound-track too, persuading me to remain faithful to my roots on whatever trajectory this search for identity might lead.

For two years before I went to Berkeley I worked for the Student Christian Movement (SCM) as Welsh Secretary. Though based at the SCM's community house in Aberystwyth, my brief was to travel throughout Wales to colleges and universities offering support to denominational groups, and seeking to nurture new groups of students who were willing to challenge traditional and often fundamentalist interpretations of Scripture, and explore ways in which the Christian faith could become a catalyst for social and political engagement – in spheres and organisations such as CND, the anti-apartheid campaign, feminism, the politics of sexuality and even party politics. I grew considerably in my understanding of my faith during these years on the SCM staff, and I'm deeply indebted to my co-workers, especially Heather, Derek, Caroline, Barry and Judith, for their friendship and example. Heather Walton became an academic and is currently Professor of Theology and Creative Practice at the University of Glasgow. Derek Whyte, after a long career in local government, is currently the Assistant Chief Executive at Preston Council. Caroline Smith became an Immigration Caseworker for one of the most diverse inner-city areas in London and her recent collection of poems, *The Immigration Handbook*, is a moving record of her work over many years. Barry Gardiner, active in party politics for decades, became influential in the Labour party in the time of Jeremy Corbyn. Judith Maizel served as a Methodist minister for thirty-six years during which time she worked for Housing Justice and as the Assistant General Secretary of Churches Together in Britain and Ireland.

These were also the years I began a life-long journey to understand myself as a spiritual being – well, if it's possible to understand spirituality. I'd lived in SCM House in Aberystwyth during my last year as an undergraduate, and for a couple of years before joining the SCM staff. Our regular obligation as a member of the community was to cook for one another and eat together – and the cook always had to offer the meal-time prayer which was sometimes just 'thanks a lot for what we've got on our plates before us'. Phil Roderick, who'd been a member of a religious community for a few years before coming to Aberystwyth to study theology, would sometimes lead Morning Prayer for a week, or offer a day of silence, a month of Evening Prayer, or an afternoon reading Psalms followed by a time of reflection on what we'd read. Because of the intermittent nature of these occasions, no one felt saddled – each member of the community could 'dip in and out' and take from the experience what they needed, or reject it with a shrug of the shoulders.

As children, my mother took Tony and me to the nearest Welsh-speaking chapel, which was Calvinistic Methodist in theology, though officially known as the Presbyterian Church of Wales. The theology wasn't important to Megan – it was all about the Welsh language, and wearing a hat, and being seen to be respectable. We were speaking both Welsh and English at home – my father understood Welsh pretty well, but he had no confidence, or will, to speak the language – so once the new television in the corner of the living room brought English to dominate our family life, she believed that chapel and Sunday school in Welsh would be good for us. My early experience of worship, then, was the hymn-prayer-sandwich with rambling extemporary prayers and a twenty minute sermon (if we were lucky and the preacher didn't get into too much of a *hwyl*)... something done to us whilst we fidgeted on uncomfortable pews. Holy Communion happened only once every three months – because it was too special to do more often like the Romans and the Anglicans – and we did it to remember Jesus's sacrifice for us – though I'm not sure I understood what that meant; perhaps one of those long-winded sermons had tried to explain it. I did know that there was such a thing as a liturgy because my father's tradition was Anglican (Church in Wales) – not that he ever went to church as an adult. During the occasional visit to St John's, the 'cathedral' up on the hill above Barmouth (a Victorian stamping of Anglicanism on a non-conformist and largely Welsh-speaking community), we'd fumble with the pages in the prayer book, the unfamiliarity of the rite making it hard to follow, the words seeming pious and other-worldly.

Morning and Evening Prayer with Phil Roderick and other members of the SCM community house were a revelation; I got to actively participate in something that we did together... I remember Phil telling us that liturgy meant 'work of the people' within worship. And so it was that Taizé chants, reading the Bible, reading both sacred and secular prose and verse, sitting in silence reflecting on what I'd read and occasionally using the Book of Common Prayer became a regular part of my weekly routine.

But 'the church', that human creation which institutionalises and controls faith and steers us into religious cul-de-sacs, I found alien and alienating. I was suspicious of the welcome on every notice board outside every chapel and church building – because as a gay man I knew I wasn't welcome… a conclusion I'd drawn from fire-and-brimstone sermons, meetings with chaplaincy and denominational groups across Wales, and the national debate within the church (of England) during the 1970s that culminated in the publication, in 1978, of *Homosexual Relationships* (more widely known as the Gloucester Report). In addressing the issue of homosexual love from a pastoral and ethical perspective, the Gloucester Report went further than earlier Anglican reports, which had primarily been about the legal status of homosexuals, and asked whether homosexual relations might not in some cases, although by no means all, be as genuine an expression of love as other human relationships? My answer was 'of course' – though at the time that was more an expression of hope than of my lived experience. There was a vociferous and snide backlash from conservative evangelicals across Britain to the possibility that gay people could form loving bonds and *Homosexual Relationships* was suppressed. I tried hard to hold on to the knowledge that there were people in 'the church' – like Huw and Mair in Aberystwyth – who were more than sympathetic to the position of gay Christians, but my response to the negativity that spewed out was to negate the church, to see it as a flawed human institution that I could live without. My attendance waned and I stopped taking communion – as a conscious act of disavowal... but at the same time I became more rooted in my own spiritual discipline.

Sometime in 1979 or 1980, on a visit to the University Anglican Chaplaincy in Bangor (as Welsh Secretary of the Student Christian Movement), the chaplain, Barry Morgan, whom I'd come to know on previous visits, asked me why I hadn't come forward at the Eucharist. I told him that as a gay man I didn't feel welcome at the table, so why would I share bread in hostile company? Forty years have passed by now, and I can't begin to paraphrase Barry's response. I recall that we talked perhaps four or five times, over the course of a year – once together with Sister Renate (from the Community of the Holy Name, an order of Anglican nuns) who was serving as assistant chaplain – and through those conversations I came to understand that even Christ's gift of himself had been 'institutionalised'... but it was, never-the-less Christ's gift, and not something that belonged to the church. So however alienated I felt from the institution, I still had an invitation to receive what was Christ's to offer. Renate asked whether I could identify with the body of Jesus, marked by wounds, and Barry challenged me to think about the presence of Jesus in the broken bread.

For some weeks I reflected on the communion service in the Book of Common Prayer and considered Barry and Renate's questions. During this time, on a brief visit to see Tony and his new wife, Kath, in Liverpool, I discovered the St Louis Jesuits. Pauline Books and Media, the Roman Catholic book shop on Bold Street, had become a regular haunt on my visits to the city and as I browsed the bookshelves, one of the sisters had put on some background music. And so, the sacred songs of John Foley, Bob Dufford, Tim Manion, Dan Schutte, Roc O'Connor and John Kavanaugh displaced the chants from Taizé for some months. Foley's *One Bread, One Body* became the background music of my days: *One bread, one body, one Lord of all, one cup of blessing which we bless. And we, though many, throughout the earth, we are one body in this one Lord*, and Renate's direct, disturbing question wove through my listening. *We are one body in this one Lord*; images of the crucified Jesus from my art history classes at school and stained glass windows in churches I'd visited became interlaced with images of being shocked in Denbigh... of being raped in a tent on Fegla Fawr... of being taunted and bullied over many years for being gay. I knew the brokenness, the wounds of persecution... but what then was my response supposed to be?

Barry's question about the presence of Jesus in the broken bread mystified me, but my curiosity about that question, and my frustration at seemingly missing Renate's point about identifying with Christ's brokenness, brought me back to the table, believing that perhaps my understanding would be nurtured by my participation.

Some years later, on Holy Hill in Berkeley, during a

semester long course in Christology – that part of theology that's concerned with Jesus's human and divine natures, his death and resurrection – we spent an entire afternoon discussing the presence of Jesus in the breaking of the bread and the pouring of the wine, that sacrament called the Eucharist. I recalled Barry's question... and as the afternoon progressed I came to understand that it's a question believers have argued over for centuries. Does the bread really become his body? Does the wine simply represent his blood? Complicated theories were expounded and explored; transubstantiation, consubstantiation, 'objective reality, but pious silence about technicalities', memorialism. Over beer and pizza at La Val's on Euclid Avenue that evening there was a lively discussion; the Roman Catholics present really did believe that the bread and wine are changed in a way beyond human comprehension into the Body, Blood, Soul, and Divinity of Christ, and yet, the bread and wine remain. The Episcopalians and the Methodists believed that in the sacrament the bread and the wine are really and truly changed into the body and the blood of Christ, but the technicalities of that process aren't important – you just believe it. I said I thought that the bread and wine were symbolic of the body and blood of Jesus, and that taking communion was a commemoration of the sacrificial death of Christ – who wasn't present in the sacrament, except in the minds and hearts of the communicants.

Slowly I came to an understanding of the Eucharist, which somehow brought together my identification with Jesus's brokenness in the breaking of the bread, as a challenge: sharing the bread and the wine became an unsettling, revolutionary act of acknowledgement that we share a common humanity which, in turn, calls each of us to respond to the face of Christ in every human being... neither Jew nor Gentile, neither slave nor free, nor is there male and female... nor homosexual... nor immigrant... nor refugee... nor junkie... nor trans. It's a discomforting thought to many – that through this sacrament we're obliged to see 'all those undesirables on whom we place labels to mark their difference from us' as those deserving of our care and compassion – deserving of our love... even deserving a place at the table.

As the only one at the communion rail in Effeld's church to receive a blessing from *Herr Pastor* Wieners, I feel special – rather than the odd-man-out; that's largely due to the different tinted glasses Dr Cindy Coleman helped me to discover in Berkeley. And there's a protestant church in Heinsberg, just twenty minutes from Effeld, when I feel the need to be reminded, through the Eucharist, that I must see Christ's face in the Seehofers and the leaders of the AfD, the Trumps, the Johnsons and Putins of this world.

And Barry Morgan and Sister Renate? I corresponded with Renate for some twenty years and always found her letters filled with joy, humour and wisdom. We met irregularly, but I was privileged to visit her once at Lambeth Palace, where, chosen by the Archbishop of Canterbury, she was ministering as a 'praying presence'. Barry became the Bishop of Bangor and later, as the Bishop of Llandaff, was elected the Archbishop of Wales, only retiring in 2017.

10

Ferry Cross the Mersey

Jupp has known Klaus and Marion for almost forty years. Whenever we visited Germany we'd always make time to be with them; perhaps an evening dinner, a walk in the park or sometimes just *Kaffee und Kuchen*. Since our arrival in Effeld we've been meeting once a month to hike in the Meinweg National Park, over the edge in the Netherlands, and to savour the delights of Dutch fast food – *frikandel speciaal*, a kind of hotdog with raw onions, and a heap of chips with mayonnaise and ketchup. This delicacy is Jupp and Klaus' favourite but the horse meat puts me off. Marion brings her friend, Marita, and sometimes the dogs come with us, but they're getting older and stiff-jointed, and Klaus, a vet, suggested that maybe they'd reached an age when a 'little and often' was better for them than a long day's trek.

Throughout these border lands there are reminders of the Second World War; sometimes a simple engraved standing stone by a footpath in the forest or the propeller of a Lancaster bomber, hauled from a boggy field, and set amongst crimson geraniums by the side of the road; in places there are even formal plaques – detailing a battle, a mass execution or simply describing the earthworks so common in the landscape. We were walking in the forest area known as Leudal. In just a few square kilometres around the villages that edge the forest, twenty aeroplanes, including Messerschmitts, Lancasters, Wellingtons and Spitfires, were downed between 1941 and 1945. Six hundred and eighty-seven people from the military of eleven nations were killed in this small pocket of land on the edge and after the war the forest communities erected a Monument of Tolerance. Jupp had read about it whilst researching his maternal grandmother's years in service with a Dutch family in one of these villages, Roggel, during and after the First World War. Sculpted by Thea Houben, from Roggel, it's a bronze half-arch standing maybe two meters high on a bed of smooth stones from the nearby river Maas, one for each of the killed. A cloud of seagulls at the apex of the half-arch represents freedom and eleven bands of coloured paving stones leading to the sculpture commemorate the eleven nationalities of the dead. We read the plaque – in Dutch, German and English; we all had the same information and we reflected in a silence... a silence that took me beyond my comfort zone.

We continued our hike and I recalled that when growing up, we were always warned not to speak about the war if there were Germans present. My mother's concern was that we might taunt the 'refugees' at the Ockenden

Venture's Hendre Hall in Barmouth, many of whom were from the families of eastern Germans displaced after the re-drawing of post-war boundaries when Germany was forced to give up land to Poland and the Soviet Union. It still surprises me that I feel uncomfortable as a Briton living in Germany when the World Wars are mentioned. I'm also surprised by how articulate many Germans are in their acknowledgement of war crimes perpetrated in the names of their parents and grandparents and I realize how I, as an inheritor of the victory, have rarely been challenged to reflect on the war crimes of the British... yet even today, the discovery of unexploded ordnance from the blanket bombing of German civilians in cities across this country is a regular occurrence, causing mass evacuations sometimes lasting a few days, whilst the ever-on-stand-by bomb disposal crews go about their business.

Walking on, I could hear Marion telling Marita about the time she and Klaus visited us in Liverpool... the two cathedrals, Roman and Anglican, at each end of a street called Hope. And my thoughts were drowned out by Gerry and the Pacemakers crossing the Mersey, an ear-worm since I'd been woken that morning by their singing on WDR4.

Two of my father's uncles had married Scousers and my grandmother – the child of an English soldier and the daughter of a Romany gypsy family that had settled in

Newtown (Montgomeryshire) and worked the canals – often went to stay with her brother Jim and his wife, Lizzie, in Birkenhead. A day out to Liverpool was an annual treat when we were children, at least until Dr Beeching savaged the railways... and then Tony had gone to medical school in Liverpool. Long considered the capital of north Wales, with a sizable Welsh speaking population, the city, then, was familiar and unthreatening, despite its rough reputation.

Within a month of my return to Wales from California, in the late summer of 1984, I interviewed for a job in Liverpool and was successful. I took up the position of Chaplain to the Merseyside Welsh at the beginning of October, a new venture funded by the Home Mission Board of the Presbyterian Church of Wales and the Liverpool Presbytery of that church. The post had been created to offer pastoral care in both Welsh and English to people from Wales who were in Liverpool for specialist hospital treatment, to the Welsh inmates in Walton gaol and to students who'd come over Offa's Dyke to study – and to conduct services a couple of times a month in the Welsh chapels that were still striving to keep open their doors. The need for such a post had arisen during the late 1970s and early 1980s with the deaths and retirements of several of the ministers of Liverpool's Welsh chapels; they and their predecessors had carried out this work for more than a century and it was neither reasonable nor practical for the one remaining minister to continue to offer such a broad ministry.

Perhaps I ought to have paid more attention to the red warning lights that flashed in my mind's eye during those first weeks in Liverpool. At twenty-eight years of age – an adult and old enough to be married with children – I didn't believe that my request for a one bedroom flat was over-reaching, but the Presbytery was paying my rent (and one of the Presbytery members was a property developer/landlord) so on my arrival in Liverpool I was offered a ground floor bed-sit. With one wall-mounted gas fire and a dubiously stained carpet in the bed-sitting-room, a sparse kitchen with cracked linoleum on the floor and a bathroom with a stained bath tub, a cracked wash basin and a toilet that hadn't seen bleach for who knew how long: it was a student fleapit. The response to my repeated appeal for a one-bedroom flat was curt: the Presbytery would monitor the progress of the new ministry and consider my request in a year. Such parsimony on the part of the Presbytery did little to assure me that I was held in much esteem. Tony, my sister-in-law Kath and I spent a long weekend cleaning and re-decorating, and I had the carpet professionally cleaned, but the stain remained... partly hidden under the new sofa-bed. Kath ran up some curtains on her electric sewing machine and Tony bought me a free-standing pine shelf unit – and looking through one set of tinted glasses they had helped me create a comfortable, if cramped home.

On my first morning in-post I met with Ben Rees, the only remaining minister in the Presbytery. He was keen that we work as a team and he handed me a list of additional Sunday services, to ease his burden, and an official Royal Liverpool Hospital ID card – with the job title of Assistant Chaplain. The red light flashed another warning. I explained that my job description was clear as to the number of Sunday services I would conduct and that my job title was Chaplain – and not anyone's assistant. Ben's response was that I needed to be flexible – and it became clear to me as the weeks passed that Ben's understanding of flexible was that I was to be malleable according to his will – after all, he'd been in ministry in Liverpool for almost 20 years. That said, what I remember most about Ben and Meinwen Rees is their kindness towards me; Meinwen's Sunday lunches were always welcome and always delicious – and I was especially appreciative of their warm hospitality during the winter months when ice patterns would form on the inside of my kitchen windows.

The red light that flashed brightest, however, was the one that signalled my own disappointment in myself. Of course, no one on the interview panel for the chaplaincy job had asked me about my sexuality... and of course, I knew that if I'd disclosed that I was gay my candidacy for the job would have been instantly dismissed. I'd chosen to withhold information, and if it ever became known, I'd be 'released' from my two-year contract. I'd chosen to re-enter the closet that I'd spent a few years in California sweeping clean... and so there was a secret to be harboured. That sense of myself that I'd come to understand with Cindy Coleman's help in Berkeley, that wonderful freedom to be me, was choked... was strangled. A new double-life had begun.

The chaplaincy work quickly gained momentum. My appointment had been widely publicised in the denominational newspaper and clergy from across north Wales (and sometimes further afield) were diligent in passing on information about their members who were in college, hospital or gaol. In the large regional cancer treatment centre at Clatterbridge Hospital there were as many as a dozen people from north Wales at any one time undergoing surgery, chemo- and/or radio-therapy, and with no prison across the north of Wales there was a significant Welsh population in HMP Liverpool in Walton. There was, then, even after just a few weeks in post, no shortage of demand for my service, and I loved the hospital and prison work. It's a rare honour and deep privilege to be with... to be alongside... a person in their sickness or their incarceration – mostly listening, perhaps holding a hand. Sometimes people wanted to talk about heaven or hell, or God's love, or even God's wrath; it was shocking to me just how many people believed that their cancer, their mental ill-health, their haemorrhoids, their stomach ulcers, their kidney stones and their heart attacks were a punishment. Trying to convince them otherwise was often futile... most people seem to need someone to blame for their misfortune and in a largely post-Christian society God seems a good-enough scapegoat. But, perhaps hedging their bets, prayers were often requested, and praying the Lord's Prayer with a convicted murderer or reciting a beloved Psalm with someone terminally ill – which often prove to be a comfort in such situations – is a profoundly humbling experience. I dug deeply into myself to resource the continuous outflow of compassion but was often exhausted, especially after prison visits. In Berkeley, during a three-month full-time hospital chaplaincy placement, I'd come to understand and appreciate the importance of regular worship and participation in liturgy in the restoration of my equilibrium and the re-charging of my batteries. Despite leading worship, often three Sundays out of four, I knew that I needed to find a church community that felt safe – a place where I could be the worshipper.

From a student handbook I'd picked up at the student's union I found a list of gay pubs and clubs and in Scarlett's one evening I got chatting with a group of men – all of whom went to church. They talked fondly about Father Colin, their priest, and how friendly the congregation at

St Margaret's was. And so I sought out Colin Oxenforth at St Margaret's on Princes Road in Toxteth, a mile or so from where I lived. We talked. Colin was straightforward, plain speaking… "We're Anglo-Catholic, and some people can't cope with the smells and bells," he said. "I say Mass every day, you're welcome to try us for size." I remember asking him about whether he believed Christ became present in the bread at the Eucharist.

"If you believe it, then he does," Colin said.

Some mornings, it was just Colin and me in the side chapel. I wondered sometimes if feeding on the sacrament had become an addiction – but it 'restored my soul'. I thanked God, too, for the wisdom of the Psalms, and together with the brothers of Taizé and the St Louis Jesuits, Henri Nouwen's *The Wounded Healer* became a constant companion in my spiritual life.

And Steven became a companion in my double life! Steve was still married, but separated from his wife of fifteen years for more than a year before I arrived in the city; she'd wanted no more to do with him after he'd come out to her as a gay man at the age of thirty-eight. She'd found another lover, but divorce proceedings had been put on hold, complicated by financial considerations, an old, infirm parent living in the granny flat and three children under twelve. They'd come to an 'arrangement'; they shared a house – but not a bed, they shared the childcare and the granny care, Steven paid the bills from his lucrative architect's practice, and they lived independent lives... at least for the time being. I saw Steven just one evening a week – for almost two years. It suited us both, indeed it was a cherished time. We'd eat lasagne in Maranto's on Lark Lane and then walk around the lake in Sefton Park. We'd go to the cinema, the theatre or the Philharmonic Hall. Sometimes we went to Scarlett's or Sadie's or the Lisburn – Liverpool's gay bars. The tabloid newspapers would have made much of the story, and surely relished in my 'downfall'. My immorality... my impropriety... would have shocked the Presbytery and the Home Mission Board – and despite how quickly they had come to appreciate and praise my 'good work' – there's little doubt in my mind that my contract would have been instantly terminated. The secrets, and those untold truths that actually constitute lies, troubled me. I was becoming someone I didn't like all over again.

But there was much that fed my ego and drove me on. The Chaplain's Office at the Royal Liverpool Hospital, a space I shared with other chaplains whom I rarely saw, was underneath the hospital chapel, and to get to the chapel you had to pass the hospital shop and a large lounge area where someone was always eating a sandwich or drinking a mug of tea from the Women's Royal Voluntary Service stall. It was here that I met Peter Carey and Chad Brown sometime towards the end of October, just weeks after I'd started my new job. Peter was one of the

Consultant Physicians in Genito-Urinary Medicine and
Chad was one of the social workers who worked in Peter's
clinic. They'd come looking for me. Chad explained that
he knew someone, who knew someone who attended one
of the Welsh chapels where I'd taken a service. In a sermon
I'd referred to my chaplaincy work in San Francisco, and
the pastoral care of terminally ill young men with AIDS.
Peter had just diagnosed his first case of AIDS and he and
Chad were eager for any information or support I might
be able to offer. Within a week I was the 'guest speaker' at
their department staff meeting. At the end of my 'talk'
there was a barrage of questions that I did my best to field
– and I found myself grateful once again that my
undergraduate studies in immunology had made it possible
for me to keep abreast with the current scientific literature
about the new mystery disease. Peter asked if I would be
available, within my chaplaincy work, to counsel and
support his patients diagnosed with AIDS. I said that I'd
have to discuss it with the Presbytery and the Mission
Board and that he'd need to give me a few days before I
could give him a response. Ben Rees didn't think it would
be a good use of my time; he was concerned that I hadn't
yet focussed on the students... he hadn't seen any increase
in student numbers at his services. Dafydd Andrew Jones,
my boss at the Mission Board in Cardiff, said that if I
thought that's what I was being called to do, I should do
it.

I met with Peter and Chad two or three times before that first Christmas in Liverpool and from those conversations, and through their contacts, a small steering group was formed with the aim of establishing a support group for people diagnosed with AIDS and a telephone help-line to offer information and advice to those who'd been scared silly by sensational tabloid journalism. And so the Merseyside AIDS Support Group (MASG) was formed, and through the following spring and early summer I helped train volunteers for the telephone service which was launched in September 1985 – the first such helpline outside London. I was hugely proud of our achievement.

The proposed work in my job description with students never really took off – and Ben never let me forget it. I made contact with more than thirty students in those first months, their details passed to me by clergy from across Wales. The few amongst them who were still regular churchgoers were enjoying the variety of experiences offered by the University Chaplaincy Services and the city churches, while those from close-knit Welsh-speaking communities who were stricken with *hiraeth* often went home for the weekend; the A55 expressway – despite a few sections still to be developed – offered speedy access and there was no shortage of students with cars posting lift offers on the notice boards in the students' union. The reality, however, was that a significant majority of those students I spoke with couldn't wait to leave Wales and experience 'the big city'... and even the 'big bad city'. In conversations, over time, with different Presbytery members, it became apparent that the student work had been added to the job description as an after-thought. Though the Welsh chapels had traditionally offered a thriving Welsh social life that new-comers to the city could tap into, like church membership in general, there'd been a gradual decline in these activities since the 1960s. A less deferential society, a nation-wide slow-burning crisis in religious belief, a rising standard of living offering more expendable income for an increasing leisure industry... all probably contributed to a significant demographic change, and by the middle of the 1980s young people from Wales coming to college in Liverpool were looking elsewhere for an exciting social life. Once I understood this, I was able to view Ben's frequent assertion to the Presbytery, that my work with students was a failure, through a different set of glasses.

I met with Dafydd Andrew Jones, the head of the Home Mission Board in Cardiff and the person I considered my boss, every couple of months – usually in Aberystwyth; there were often meetings there that he had to attend and it was only a couple of hours drive from Liverpool. I'd always found our discussions helpful... and challenging... and I was grateful that he listened – and that he seemed to hear what I was saying, which wasn't always the case in the Presbytery. My two-year contract was about to end and we'd agreed over the phone to discuss the future of the chaplaincy – and whether I'd come to any decision about ordination, something he'd encouraged me to reflect upon and pray about at every one of our meetings... "... because the church needs people like you", he'd said so often.

I liked Dafydd Andrew, so I came out to him... it was the only way I could honestly explain why I couldn't go ahead with the ordination process. I was sick of leading a double life, and lying through my teeth to jump through the hoops of the ordination process would have made me hate myself – and I doubted that the Presbyterian Church of Wales was open to ordaining an openly gay man. I remember that his response was full of empathy; he said that he respected my integrity and conceded that he better understood my passion for the AIDS work – and that if that's what I believed God was calling me to do then it was a noble and valid ministry to pursue... as a lay person. We didn't discuss renewing my contract. On the first of October 1986 I signed on, becoming one of Maggie's millions.

I treated Steven badly. At the time he seemed so much a part of my secret, double life – which was no longer necessary or desirable. The restrictions on both our lives in the previous years had led me to work hard not to fall in love with him. But he'd fallen in love with me. As I prepared to stride off into a new life, Steve offered to divorce his wife, sort out his finances and set up home with me. But I walked away.

II

Bohemian Rhapsody

In general, the Dutch don't dub foreign language television or films; it's one of the reasons so many of them speak three or four languages so fluidly; indeed, the pervasiveness of English has sparked growing concern in the Netherlands that Dutch is being pushed aside, especially in university education at post-graduate level. We go regularly to the multiplex cinema in Roermond, the large Dutch city over the edge, just twenty minutes from Effeld. It doesn't help my German to watch films in English, but when characters' lips are not in synchrony with their voice-over I get distracted and hearing the likes of Judy Dench and Rhys Ifans speaking German is just silliness. Jupp and I both like Queen and it was Freddy Mercury that tickled our interest in opera with his Olympic duet with Montserrat Caballé – Barcelona! Barcelona! We quickly became opera queens after that. The Queen bio-pic, *Bohemian Rhapsody*, was thrilling, but it churned up memories of the early days of AIDS.

It was Alan Schut, who worked in the Dean of Students' office at Pacific School of Religion in Berkeley, who first alerted me to the mysterious disease that was killing gay men. Alan met me on my arrival at San Francisco airport – a welcome delegation of one... 'After all, you're this year's WCC Scholar'. The drive to Berkeley took us on an elevated stretch of freeway high above San Francisco onto the four and a half mile long Bay Bridge; and as I marvelled at the city laid out below us, he suggested – knowing that the submission I'd made for the scholarship was to do with pastoral responses to lesbians and gay men – that I might want to consider how all the agencies in the city, and not just the churches, were responding to the tragedy that had begun to ravage the gay community causing disfigurement and disability... and untimely death.

"It hasn't even got a name yet," Alan said when I questioned him. "It's a whole collection of symptoms – a hacking cough that won't go away, and some guys get bruises all over their body, little black blotches the size of a nickel, and thrush and herpes and god-awful diarrhoea."

Neither of us knew, as we drove across the bay to Berkeley, that the hacking cough young gay men were developing was caused by a rare lung infection called *Pneumocystis carinii* pneumonia (PCP) and the nickel-sized bruising had been diagnosed as an unusually aggressive cancer named Kaposi's sarcoma. Both are indicative of a break down in the body's immune system, allowing a range of infections to take hold – a syndrome of infections. It would be almost a year later, in June 1982, before a research cluster of cases among gay men in southern California suggested that the cause of the immune deficiency was linked to gay sex and the syndrome was initially called gay-related immune deficiency or GRID. However, the Centres for Disease Control and Prevention (CDC), the leading national public health institute of the United States with headquarters in Atlanta, Georgia, had already received notifications of severe immune deficiency amongst a group of haemophiliacs in Haiti and amongst injecting drug users in cities around the US, and in September 1982 they used the term Acquired Immune Deficiency Syndrome – AIDS – for the first time. With heightened awareness amongst the medical community around the world, cases of AIDS began to be reported from across the globe, and as early as January 1983 the female partners of men with AIDS, particularly in Africa, were reported with the syndrome, which strongly suggested that sexual transmission between men and women was as likely as between two men. And yet, AIDS became known as 'the gay plague' and homosexual men who'd 'come out' and found refuge from harassment and discrimination – and solidarity – in the 'gay communities' of the large cities in western Europe and north America were vilified... scape-goated... hounded... sending many back into the closet. The fear amongst gay men became febrile – as did a sense of denial; it can't happen to someone like me.

My first months in Berkeley were a heady mix of excitement; a new life in a different culture, making new friends, an academic challenge that sometimes made me doubt myself... and then, once I'd started to see Cindy Coleman, some deep personal pain and self-discovery. Alan Schut would sometimes pass me a copy of the *Bay Area Reporter* or the *Advocate* with an article about AIDS, but the unfolding story of a global public health tragedy was something only in the background of my awareness.

The many weeks of electric shock aversion therapy in Denbigh in 1975 had rendered me fearful that any sexual response I experienced would trigger flashbacks so I'd worked hard in the intervening years to block such feelings. The forays into sexual relationships in Aberystwyth, the fling with Dafydd Owen and the year of misery with Bob Harney, had left me convinced that celibacy was my only valid option – but more through circumstances than through vocation. In trying to unlearn the outcomes of Dafydd Alun Jones's crude attempts to re-orientate my sexuality, my conversations with Cindy were frequently sexually explicit. She asked me, quite early in our time together, to explore my body by touch – to re-connect with my physical self... and my sexual self, and keep a diary of any sexual responses – but not to masturbate... that might come later. I'd share my journal jottings with her every week and often torrents of anger would overflow – mostly directed at 'what happened in Denbigh'. Cindy suggested that I write a letter to the doctors and nurses in the asylum back in Wales – as honest a response as I felt able to offer... even if it was filled with hatred and vitriol. The letter I wrote was indeed a tirade of profanity and loathing for what 'they' had done to me; it was never sent – I don't believe Cindy ever intended for me to send it – but it did open a channel for the flow of bitterness and resentment that I'd come to harbour. I forget how many weeks I beat-up the floor cushion in Cindy's office, thumping hell out of Dr D A Jones and his helpers... and then one day – from a deep recess in my psyche, the face of the man from the tent on Fegla Fawr – and I punched, and punched; I even drove to one of the deserted beaches north of the San Francisco bay, and screamed and yelled – and told Dr Jones... and my rapist, exactly what I thought of them.

I'd be telling a lie if I claimed here that any sense of release was immediate or that forgiveness came easily, but by the spring of 1982 – four or five months after I'd started seeing Cindy – I began to sense a lightness and an internal calm which was new... and my sexual desire seemed to re-awaken. I was going-on 26, and like a teenager I'd find myself attracted to men at random on the street or get an erection sitting next to a man on the tram, excited by his closeness, his smell, the rhythm of his breathing. I wrote about it in my diary and talked it through with Cindy. "So maybe it's time to explore masturbation," she said. "You might even fantasize about those men in the street or the man on the tram." I did, and there were no flash-backs.

For my twenty-sixth birthday I treated myself; I went to The Steamworks, the gay bathhouse on Fourth Street in Berkeley. I wanted to be naked amongst men. I wasn't looking for sex; I wasn't ready for that – and fairly anonymous 'recreational sex', which seemed to be commonplace in such saunas, wasn't something I'd envisaged or desired. I just wanted to touch, and be touched... no more than that, really. I struck up a conversation with a man in the steambath; he was from Argentina. We were both embarrassed by the war between our countries over the Malvinas/Falklands... and shocked that the day before, Thatcher had ordered the sinking of the General Belgrano. He touched my thigh and asked me what I 'liked'. I stroked his chest and said that I just wanted to cuddle. He laughed and asked what kind of 'quaint English sexual practice' that was, and he laughed again when I explained that I didn't want to have sex with him, but just to hug. So we hugged. And after a while we kissed. And there were no flash-backs. And then I thanked him – and walked away... fully aware that we were both sexually aroused. I'll always remain grateful to him for his patience, his sense of humour and his warmth.

Cindy was taken aback when I read her my diary. "They're dangerous places now, with this disease. Please tell me you won't do anything to put yourself at risk."

"Unless kissing and cuddling are a risk..." I began, but she interrupted.

"Does anyone really know yet what's causing it? Just be careful, that's all I'm saying. Haven't you got a gay friend you could be naked with... to explore with you?"

"But that's just not logical, Cindy. What might a stranger in a bathhouse have done that one of my gay friends, confident enough and willing to be naked with me, might not have done? And besides, I'm clear about my boundaries."

But my boundaries became blurred. Some weeks later, on a return visit to The Steamworks, I hugged and kissed for a while with a man I recognized from the previous semester's Old Testament class. Then we touched one another intimately and there were glorious fireworks. In my diary I wrote that *we got into some heavy petting – nothing more, I suppose, than what many teenagers might get up to once they've been on a couple of dates*. I'd had an orgasm with a man and there were no flash-backs. At twenty-six, I'd unlearned enough of the negative conditioning about being gay to find joy and pleasure in sex – with a man... and I liked it.

I could easily understand the addictive lure of places like The Steamworks but I wondered, too, just how satisfying such fleeting liaisons could be. I don't think I thought too much about casual sex in moral terms – two consenting adults were sharing some pleasure for a couple of hours, just like two people might go out for dinner or watch a play or a film. But because my two visits had helped me to re-claim what aversion therapy had tried to erase, I felt free enough to think about finding a boyfriend... and so it was that between Christmas and New Year in 1982 I met and fell in love with Michael Wyatt.

Michael was on the re-bound. He was honest about it. He'd been in a relationship with a man for three years, but his lover had been a sex addict, sometimes spending two or three evenings a week in San Francisco's bathhouses. They'd finally split up at the end of the summer, but he was still raw. We decided 'to date' for a while and not rush into sex. I think we dated for – about three weeks.

The first man I met whom I knew to have AIDS was Bill Palmatier, the organist at the church where I served as an assistant minister during my final year in seminary – until my graduation in May 1984. I only knew Bill in the last months of his life – as a sick man. Members of the congregation at Bethany United Methodist Church in San Francisco often talked about his energy and his enthusiasm for church music, his sometimes caustic humour, his generosity with both his time and his money

– and how handsome he had been. The man I met had sunken cheeks with eyes that looked too big and teeth too prominent. The lesions of Kaposi's sarcoma on his face were sometimes masked with foundation cream, but then his skin looked blotchy because the cream hadn't been smoothed and blended-in... and without the foundation his cheeks and forehead were spotted black and blue. His lips were frequently swollen and scabby from herpes, his voice hoarse from coughing. The minister at Bethany, Chris Shiber had just had her first pregnancy confirmed, and because of the speculation, sometimes bordering on hysteria, about how whatever caused AIDS might be casually transmitted, she was reluctant to visit Bill, which is how I – the new kid on the block – came to be visiting him, both in the hospital and in his home. On communion Sundays, immediately after the service, I'd take Bill the consecrated bread and wine; sometimes we'd recite prayers from the Episcopal prayer book, the tradition of his childhood, and sometimes we'd sit in silence. Bill never asked me directly to hold his hand – he'd always say, "Would you mind if I held your hand?" If I visited him on a weekday I'd often find him listening to music – he liked Simon and Garfunkel, and Elton John... and he often had Joan Armatrading singing *Willow* on repeat – *Shelter in a storm*.

After the first time Bill held my hand I got swept up in a wave of panic... as if his touch had flicked the switch in my mind that forced me to fit together the pieces of the AIDS jigsaw I had already gleaned from scientific journals at the university library. Already, in May 1983, French scientists had isolated a virus they believed was the cause of the immune deficiency – a virus which had probably been circulating in the human population for decades with the potential to remain dormant in an individual for long periods before its destructive capabilities were triggered... and which was probably blood-borne and sexually transmitted. Indeed, those currently showing symptoms of AIDS may have been non-symptomatic, infectious carriers for years.

The first ripples of alarm washed over me as I drove home to Berkeley from Bill's apartment near Golden Gate Park, challenging my arrogant assumption that it couldn't happen to me. There was no opportunity to pull-over on the Bay Bridge and as the insidious notions about contagion and dormancy percolated, I concentrated on my breathing and reminded myself that the face of Christ was under that blotchy foundation cream, scarred by Kaposi's sarcoma. The full flood of anxiety and fear engulfed me after I'd parked the car and walked the few hundred yards to my apartment on campus.

I stood under the shower for more than an hour trying to rub away Bill's touch, knowing that I was behaving irrationally... but all cogent thought was being pushed aside by possibility. Could I already be infected? Through

Michael? He'd been honest enough about his ex – who had been addicted to casual sex in San Francisco's bathhouses. And what about my own visits to The Steamworks... or even the man in the tent on Fegla Fawr all those years ago who'd ejaculated into my bruised and bleeding anus?

My experiences with Bill, and the other mostly young men with AIDS I met at San Francisco General Hospital, touched my life in profound ways. I learned to live with the possibility that I was infected and 'adjusted' my behaviours to ensure I wouldn't pass on the infection, if it was present (or indeed get infected if 'it' was not already circulating in my blood). I learned to value 'the moment' and not put off until tomorrow... and banished all thoughts that 'wished my life away'. And I came to realize, and appreciate the responsibility I had to stand tall in the face of ignorance, prejudice, discrimination and hatred and speak my truth quietly and clearly, often wondering where courage was nurtured. Perhaps it was these qualities that television journalists and film makers found engaging.

By the time I returned to Britain in the late summer of 1984, the Welsh language television channel, S4C, had been broadcasting for almost two years and many of my contemporaries from secondary school and university had found jobs in television. Dilys Morris Jones, with whom I'd grown up in Barmouth, was working with *Y Byd ar*

Bedwar, the weekly current affairs programme, which had already gained a reputation for hard-hitting, investigative journalism of the highest standard. Through Dilys, I was introduced to Russell Isaac, one of the programme's journalist/presenters, and director, Phil Lewis; they wanted to make a documentary about AIDS in San Francisco... and I, a Welsh man who'd just returned from that city, had a story to share that they could use. After some months of discussion and negotiation, I travelled back to California in August 1986 to make the film, which aired later that autumn.

It's difficult to estimate the impact of the film. Prior to its broadcast, the press in Wales had barely given AIDS any column inches but at the Welsh press awards, later that year, *Y Byd ar Bedwar* was commended for its sensitive handling of difficult topics – and particularly of AIDS – which had led to informed and responsible press coverage that had challenged many of the myths pedalled by the national tabloids. For me, in the months – years even – after the film was screened, I was recognized in Wales as 'the man in the AIDS documentary', and television and radio journalists, mostly for the Welsh language services, came knocking at my door when they needed someone to talk about 'sensitive' issues related to sex and sexuality.

12

Taizé Chants –
and Nuclear Weapons

I don't attend mass with Jutta regularly. On a rainy Saturday evening, more often than not, we'll get a phone call; Gerda will have set Jutta's hair in the morning – a weekly ritual – and not wanting the rain to 'spoil' her lacquered coiffure, she'll cadge a lift. Sometimes we sing Taizé chants – and today, as the unsteady line of geriatrics lurched towards the communion rail, it was *Laudate omnes gentes*. I'd sung these words from Psalm 117 many times whilst listening to my recordings of Taizé's chanting monks, and this evening I was pulled back to the protests outside the Lawrence Livermore Laboratory, a nuclear weapons research facility about forty minutes from Berkeley... and a look-alike California cop from one of Dr Dafydd Alun Jones' pornography magazines.

The protests at Livermore were long established by the time I arrived in Berkeley in September 1981. As the weeks passed I came to realize that an arrest at Livermore was a badge of honour amongst all left-leaning seminary students at the Graduate Theological Union on Berkeley's Holy Hill – but one I would necessarily have to forego: my J1 visa status as a visiting scholar of the World Council of Churches would be jeopardised by such an infringement of the law. Despite many an invitation, I always declined the opportunity to protest Ronald Reagan's nuclear weapons machine.

During the spring of 1984 I was working a half-time internship at Bethany United Methodist Church in Noe Valley, San Francisco, as the assistant minister. For some years the churches in the Bay Area had been protesting at Livermore as part of their Lenten witness and during coffee hour after Sunday worship at the beginning of Lent a small group of Bethany's congregation decided they'd like to participate in the Good Friday prayer vigil outside the nuclear lab. The Episcopal Diocese and the northern California Conference of the United Methodist Church had secured permission to hold the prayer vigil outside a disused gate at the huge nuclear weapons facility and the protest was intended to be more symbolic than purposefully disruptive. With this in mind I agreed to go.

Friday 20 April was a warm, sunny day. Some hundreds of us were gathered before the 'disused gate' and the chant, *Laudate omnes gentes*, seemed to have taken on a life of its own, swelling and abating, as if some celestial choir director kept wanting more. And then the police moved in on us...

and the television cameras – the TV companies having been forewarned that the bishops present would be arrested.

There was no melee; everyone was good-natured and some of the police officers even joined the chant, which had swelled again as though to defy the imposition of the law. I was perhaps twenty feet away from the purple shirts who were being hand-cuffed, and fearing my own arrest I made my way toward the rear of the crowd – only to find my way blocked by more than six feet of California beefcake handsomeness; blond hair, blue-green eyes, perfect teeth that must have cost thousands of dollars and muscles bulging through shirt sleeves that attested to hours in the gym. I was disconcerted. He looked familiar. Was I about to be arrested? Would I be deported just weeks before my graduation?

"Are we all going to be detained?" I asked.

He shrugged his shoulders.

"But we're not actually causing any inconvenience... we've had permission to pray outside these gates."

"I guess it will look good on the evening news, these clergy being arraigned," he said. "You're not American... you're accent is...," he looked inquisitive.

"My accent is Welsh."

"My family came from Whales," he said, smiling broadly. "I'm third generation but there are still come cousins in Whales, near Swan-sea."

"I can't be arrested," I said, perhaps too deliberately. "My visa..." I said, throwing up my hands.

"Perhaps I'll just take down your name and address," he said, smiling. "And your phone number." And I wasn't too shaken to recognise that he was flirting... and an image from one of the pornography magazines the doctors had used in the hospital in Denbigh came to mind – a half-naked California Highway Patrol Officer making love to his motorbike.

Only six people were arrested outside the Lawrence Livermore Laboratory on that April morning. The porn-star-look-alike police officer didn't phone me. I've always wondered whether he'd passed my details to the immigration service.

13

WDR4 – Falling In Love Again

Ich bin von Kopf bis Fuß
Auf Liebe eingestellt
Denn das ist meine Welt
Und sonst gar nichts
Das ist, was soll ich machen,
Meine Natur
Ich kann halt lieben nur
Und sonst gar nichts

We wake up to Marlene Dietrich who is *Falling In Love Again*. It's a bleak December morning; in Effeld we can have grey, overcast days – even grey overcast weeks when there's no glimpse of blue sky and the sun seems lost for ever. On such days, our bedroom, painted white, feels cold, and we snuggle under the over-stuffed down duvet and try to postpone our emergence into the grey. The morning's news, sounding muffled under the thick quilt, is all about who will replace Angela Merkel. Germany's centre-right Christian Democratic Union (CDU) party is about to choose a new leader from among Friedrich

143

Merz, Jens Spahn, and Annegret Kramp-Karrenbauer. Jupp wonders how an openly gay man, Jens Spahn – the Health Minister – can be such a conservative, and find support amongst Germany's conservative seniors who make up most of the party membership. I wonder how anyone can pronounce the only female contender's name... "They call her AKK," Jupp says. The CDU has been the natural party of government for most of Germany's post-war period – and that remains the party's self-perception. But the reality is very different as the general election in 2017 and state elections during the last year saw significant party losses to the Greens and the rise of Germany's far right *Alternative für Deutschland*. And then Marlene is singing again, this time in German – *Ich bin von Kopf bis Fuß*....

I met Jupp Korsten at the beginning of December 1986. As I write, we celebrate thirty-two years together – which is incomprehensible, given the circumstances of our first encounter.

I'd been on the dole for a couple of months, since the contract with the Presbyterian Church of Wales had not been renewed. In the first weeks of being out-of-work I walked a lot around the lake in Sefton Park. I was uneasy about being unemployed – even my 'fall-back-position' as a trained teacher didn't offer much consolation... with the AIDS backlash, was any school about to employ an openly gay man? I was troubled, too, by the way I'd treated Steven and more than once considered seeing him again, but the sense that he was part of the double life I had left behind grew stronger, and as the certainty in re-discovering my equilibrium was restored, getting back in touch with him became less of an option. Most mornings I drank coffee in Keith's Wine Bar on Lark Lane, just around the corner from my bed-sit, and scoured *The Guardian* jobs section. I often slept in the afternoon, a consequence perhaps of having 'let go' of the chaplaincy and being overwhelmed by how exhausting the work had been... and there were job application forms to fill in – and sometimes a need to tailor my CV to fit the post I was applying for, which in pre-word-processing days involved a couple of hours at the manual typewriter. I went often to Mass at St Margaret's in Toxteth, usually walking the mile and a half from home, and became a regular at the Sunday ten-thirty service. Then, in early November, I was invited to interview for a position in the Public Health Department of a nearby Health Authority – one of the new HIV education and prevention posts created across Britain with ring-fenced funding Margaret Thatcher's administration had released to 'tackle the spread of AIDS'. I was confident that I'd interviewed well; I was confident, too, that with a degree in Immuno-biology, hands-on experience of working with people with AIDS in San Francisco, and my contribution to establishing the Merseyside AIDS Support Group, I was the best qualified of the candidates. After an uncomfortable two-day wait I heard that I'd got the job and heaved a huge sigh of relief; being one of 'Maggie's millions' for a few weeks hadn't been a financial hardship for me, but knowing that my savings would see me through to my first pay-day eased the nagging anxiety.

After receiving the letter from the Health Authority confirming that my employment would begin on the first Monday in January 1987, I relaxed into the luxury of free time. I slept-in until past ten some days... I read crime novels... I watched afternoon television... I gained access to the medical library at the university through Tony, my surgeon brother, and spent time reading whatever I could find in the medical and scientific journals about HIV and AIDS in preparation for the challenge ahead – I even volunteered more time on the Merseyside AIDS Support Group help-line. And I went clubbing.

Of the few gay bars and clubs in Liverpool, Scarlett's was my favourite. In the basement of an office building close to Liverpool City Hall, it was a relaxed and intimate space where thirty people made for a crowd. And it was here that I first met Jupp – not that I paid him much attention. He was with a swarthy Catalan, Ramon, to whom I was instantly attracted. We were a group of five or six around a table and as the conversations between us moved back and forth I had moments when I simply observed; it was obvious that Jupp was interested in the

Catalan too. I chatted with the man sitting next to me – Peter, and I learned that he, Ramon and Jupp were in a year-long student exchange programme; they each taught their home language in school placements around the city and together attended classes in English to gain their Cambridge Certificate of Proficiency. Any thoughts of pursuing my attraction and interest in Ramon waned; Jupp had the daily access and opportunity that I didn't.

Some days later, after a busy couple of hours on the AIDS help-line, I went 'for a quick half' to Scarlett's with a couple of the other volunteers who'd been folding leaflets in readiness for another volunteer training day. Both Ramon and Jupp were there, but at different tables. Drinks in hand, we edged towards the alcove table where Ramon appeared to be holding court, his English almost fluent. He smiled, moved into the corner of the nook and patted the space on the bench beside him. There was space for two and we were three; we looked at one another and they both smiled and said they had friends at the bar. I sat next to Ramon, wondering if... hoping that... I had a chance. The conversation that I broke into was about sexually transmitted diseases! One of the men at the table was talking about his one experience of 'the clap', and how embarrassed he'd been when visiting the doctor. Ramon said he was still recovering from hepatitis-B, which is why he was drinking cola and not having sex with anybody. So my hopes were dashed.

When the men at Jupp's table got up to leave, Jupp

pushed into the space on the bench beside me; it was a tight squeeze and his thigh nestled against mine. The conversation had moved on; Ramon was talking about a day trip he had made to north Wales – and how beautiful it was around Llangollen – which he had difficulty pronouncing. I said that I came from Wales and that if he'd like to visit the northwest coast I'd be happy to act as tour-guide. Yes... I had a car.

"Can you give me a lift home?" Ramon asked.

"Depends which part of the city you live in," I said. "I live near Sefton Park."

"That's no good for me," Ramon said, "but Jupp lives on Parkfield Road."

"Me too," I offered with some surprise.

"You could take Jupp home then," Ramon said. I wasn't sure if he was trying to fix us up.

It took us only twenty minutes to drive from the city centre. I discovered that he was German, confounding my assumption that he was Dutch. His English was poor and he was worried he wouldn't get the Cambridge Proficiency certificate at the end of the academic year... and he'd only just come out; he'd lived with a woman in Germany for five years but they'd broken up that past spring, which was what had spurred him on to apply for a year abroad... and being in England, and using a different language, had offered him the freedom to finally acknowledge what he'd known for a long time.

I dropped him off some fifty yards from the once-grand gates to the once-grand Victorian villa that was number 26 Parkfield Road, where my ground floor bed-sit opened directly onto an over-grown back garden. Readying myself for bed I reflected on human attraction – physical, sexual, spiritual. With Ramon there had been an instant spark – of lust, I supposed. With Jupp there was just a sense that I wanted to see him again. I smelled of cigarette smoke – these were the days before smoking bans in public places. Sitting in the empty bath tub, a trickle of water from the rubber shower hose attachment that didn't properly fit the taps providing an excuse for a shower, I sang – *Ich bin von Kopf bis Fuß*... and smiled as I recalled the lip-synching drag queen from Sadie's Bar Royal. It was the only German I knew... but I hoped to get to know another one.

Jupp was tucking in to a full-English when I arrived at Keith's Wine Bar the next morning. I'd never seen him there before and I took it as a sign that we were meant to meet again.

"You'll get clogged arteries if you have breakfasts like that too often," I said with a smile.

"Just once a week... on a Friday; I don't teach and I don't have a class until this afternoon," he said. "Come and sit with me."

That Friday morning in Keith's on Lark Lane marks the beginning of our long life together – the fifth of

December 1986. Jupp moved in to my cramped bed-sit on his return from the Christmas holidays, which he spent with his family in Germany, exactly four weeks to the day from that breakfast.

14

Welsh Boys Too

I'm a bit of a social media addict. Every morning I check my 'memories' and today there was a flash from the past, from Australia; already ten years ago, one of my virtual friends had just finished reading *Crawling Through Thorns*. His comments were generous and I remember being somewhat awed that someone on the other side of the world had read one of my books. Writing: it still surprises me that I write; it's a strange gift to offer someone who struggled to decipher the letters that make up words for such a long time and didn't read a novel until required to do so for O-level English.

By the spring of 1991 I was beginning to feel burnt-out. I'd been working in Public Health for four years, riding the roller-coaster of HIV prevention, in jobs that were both physically and emotionally demanding, but hugely rewarding. For a couple of years, working for the Health Promotion Unit of one of Liverpool's Area Health Authorities, I ran workshops on HIV awareness for professionals; half-days, whole-days, even two and three-days, depending on the groups involved: Social services care workers, teachers, undertakers, Catholic Social Services, the clergy of Liverpool Anglican Diocese, staff at Walton Prison, adoption and fostering services... even senior nursing officers from all the hospitals – who should have known better than to trust what they'd read in the *Daily Mail*, *The Sun* and *The Daily Mirror*. The hysteria about AIDS, whipped up by the tabloid press in Britain, had left so many confused and fearful. Funeral directors were refusing to offer their services to bereaved families whose loved one's death was AIDS-related; head teachers wanted assurances that they would be told if a haemophiliac child at their school had HIV – "...but what about your sexually active teachers... or even your senior students?" I quizzed, "do you want to know their status?"; home-helps refused to attend the homes of people known to be sick and disabled by AIDS; priests withheld communion from people they thought might be infected; Liverpool hospitals decided that all 'AIDS victims' would be cared for at the Infectious Diseases Unit at Fazakerley Hospital, with little thought about the possibility – even the likelihood – that there were non-symptomatic HIV carriers amongst both the staff and the patients in any one hospital at any one time. Over some 20 months, from March 1987, with sometimes four workshops a week and as many as thirty participants at each session, more than four thousand people were helped to quash the myths they harboured, understand some basic facts, and challenged to recognize – and believe – that they would be as safe as their own 'good practice', whatever their profession – because in most people's everyday working life we didn't 'allow' others to bleed into our own open wounds, and whatever our personal life choices, any unprotected sex we might have would hopefully, and usually be by mutual consent.

And then I was pulled from the Health Promotion Unit. The director of the Community Health Department, who had often taken the trouble to seek me out and personally commend the work I was doing, decided I should work under the direct management of one of her general managers; we would set up a new HIV prevention service working directly with injecting drug users, the community drug teams, the sexual health services and the prostitutes working along the Liverpool Dock Road, and we'd lead a campaign on safer sex for sexually active young people, both gay and straight. The new service was to be funded from ring-fenced HIV prevention funds released by Thatcher's administration; my budget was in the hundreds of thousands and my salary almost doubled.

We were a team of two, Glenys Marriott and me; we got on well together, our skills, knowledge and experience complementing one another, and we were both willing to make decisions that seemed right 'in the moment', even if that meant sticking our necks out. Within six months

Glenys, who'd had careers as a police officer and a social worker before moving into public health, had set up two new Community Drug Teams – in Kirkby and Walton, to complement and expand the work of the existing team in Waterloo, and an additional two hundred chaotic heroin addicts were brought into counselling and prescribed Methadone. I employed six outreach workers to work in pairs in these three districts – on the streets and in pubs, clubs, parks and bus shelters – to draw chaotic drug users into the new services, to provide needle and syringe exchange services to those users not yet ready or willing to enter the prescribing programme, to offer safer sex advice and condoms to the sex workers and, when necessary, provide swift access to the sexual health clinic... and to liaise with local community leaders, to help them understand this Harm Reduction approach to preventing the spread of HIV.

In these outer-lying neighbourhoods of greater Liverpool there were no gay pubs and clubs on which to focus work with gay men, but there were a number of public places where men met to have casual and relatively anonymous sex with other men. Often married with families, these men did not identify or understand themselves as gay, and in the jargon of public health promotion they were known as 'men who have sex with men', to distinguish them from gay men, because their public health needs were different. After consultation with the police, who'd often used 'pretty police' – handsome young officers – to entrap men in such public sex venues, their understanding of the need to do HIV prevention work developed rapidly and they gave assurances that the outreach teams could work without police interference... unless there were specific complaints about men importuning sex, in which case they would intervene.

The outreach teams gave condoms to anyone who wanted them. I've always maintained that there's no such thing as a 'free condom' – someone had to buy them! My budget for condoms peaked at £55k per annum, an indication of just how much potentially unsafe sexual behaviour there was within our communities.

The philosophy of Harm Reduction and Risk Minimisation was not without its opponents. At a public meeting to explain why Glenys and I had decided to open a 'health promotion shop' on Stanley Road in Bootle I was threatened. I'd employed two more people to staff the new drop-in centre, where used needles and syringes could be exchanged, where injecting drug users could get advice on infected injecting sites, and even be referred to the one local rehabilitation centre if they felt ready for the challenge to get clean. It was a safe place where prostitutes from the Dock Road could get a hot drink, pick up their condoms, and if necessary, get an immediate referral to the sexual health services. During a rowdy question time, I was challenged by a local evangelical minister who, somehow, knew something of my history with the chaplaincy. He wanted to know why I was involved 'in helping such satanic scum in their depravity'.

"Because in each of their faces I see the face of Christ," I heard myself saying, despite making great efforts to avoid using such explicitly Christian language and concepts in my secular role. "And what we're offering are the stepping stones towards the restoration of their dignity and self-worth."

There was considerable hostile opposition to our work in Bootle, members of the community believing that such a service would bring 'undesirables' in from other areas of the city. Explaining that the outreach teams had gathered sufficient evidence of a large drug using population within the Bootle area to warrant the establishment of the drop-in centre fell on deaf ears – and one angry resident suggested that I keep looking over my shoulder... a 'violent end' would come sooner rather than later. So fear became a part of my every-day life for a while – until the open-door policy of the drop-in, the frequent visits by local community leaders, and the charm and friendliness of the staff I had employed, helped to quell the anxieties that had been so virulently expressed.

During these years, in the late 1980s, there was considerable re-organisation within Liverpool's health services and by 1991 all the area's community health services were to be brought together. I took the opportunity afforded by this reorganisation not to gain advancement within the newly formed service: I was tired... the internal politics in the city-centre, especially in the drug treatment field, intimidated me... I still looked over my shoulder when I parked my car, especially at night, and when I really allowed myself to reflect on the management role I seemed to have drifted into, I was mostly not enjoying my working days.

My regular attendance at St Margaret's during this time had been nurturing, and this was probably a major contributory factor to the calmness of my temperament in my work life, often in the face of difficult situations warranting difficult decisions. My unflappability was something that drew comments from my co-workers... though I shouldn't underestimate the sense of balance and fulfilment Jupp brought to my life either. At church, Father Colin encouraged me to be confirmed in the Anglican tradition – a number of people in the congregation had suggested to him that I might take on some lay ministry role, and over a beer in Scarlett's one evening he explained that unless I became an Anglican he wouldn't be able to draw on my pastoral gifts at St Margaret's. So, I was confirmed... and I trained as a Reader, and after being granted a licence by the bishop I was soon preaching regularly.

Through the HIV awareness work I'd carried out over

a six month period for all the clergy of the Liverpool Anglican Diocese, I was invited to become Bishop David Sheppard's advisor on HIV and AIDS. For some reason, however – that no one could explain to me, the bishop felt he needed to know my HIV status before confirming my appointment. I despaired, for hadn't I emphasised, in all of the workshops that I'd run for the diocese and elsewhere, that a person's HIV status was a piece of confidential information that no one had the right to ask for – a piece of information that no one needed to 'keep themselves safe'. My response to the bishop was that my HIV status was not something I was willing to share with him.

Dr Paul Neener, a surgeon before he became a priest, was appointed the bishop's adviser on AIDS. Paul and I knew one another – he'd been one of my mentors during my training as a Reader. He wasn't wholly comfortable that the bishop had side-lined me, and before his meetings with Bishop Sheppard, he'd invite me for lunch or supper so that we could go over the agenda the bishop had set for their next meeting and discuss any new issues that seemed constantly to arise in the unfolding tragedy that is AIDS.

I started looking for a new job in the spring of 1991. Jupp had expressed his willingness to move from Liverpool despite only recently securing a full-time lecturer's position at John Moores University, but something that interested me came up in Wales – with the community health services in the north east, leading on a sexual health promotion project. Based in Mold, the new job would mean that I could commute and Jupp could pursue his academic career in the Department of Modern Languages... and if the commute proved arduous we could perhaps move to the Wirral.

On paper, the job in Wales looked fascinating. So much energy was put into health promotion work that only focussed on seeking to enhance the personal skills of individuals, to enable them to make healthy lifestyle choices, with no reference to the public policy of the day or the communities and environments in which those individuals lived. An example of this was the work I'd done with the Education Department of the Local Authority in north Liverpool; I'd attempted to enable teachers to teach about safer sex in a situation where government education policy forbade teaching about homosexuality because of Section 28 of the Local Government Act 1988, and where individual school sex education policies limited the ability of teachers to respond to students' actual anxieties and needs around exploring sexual behaviours in a safe way. The Welsh job was clear that helping to build healthy public policy and helping to create supportive environments within which individuals could choose healthier behaviours was implicit, and that excited me.

I was called for interview, but before attending I requested a meeting with the Director of Public Health of the Clwyd Area Health Authority (which was in its last months of existence due to the reorganisation of health services across Wales). I wanted to know the nature of the needs assessment work that had been done in the creation of such an ambitious job specification – or whether what was written on paper was wishful thinking. The Director was approaching retirement and within moments of being ushered into his office I got the sense that he was already one foot out of the door. He explained that the funding for the post was the same ring-fenced monies that funded my work in Liverpool, "...but here in north Wales we're not likely to see much of this AIDS so we've made it a general sexual health post," he said.

"So – do you have any clear idea about the activity of sex workers in the area... is it mostly on the streets with curb crawlers?"

"You mean prostitutes?"

"Yes... in Liverpool my outreach workers do a lot of safer sex work with sex workers."

"There might be some... up in Rhyl," he said, with a dismissive wave of his hand.

"Okay... and what about unwanted pregnancy and abortion rates?"

"This authority doesn't carry out terminations," he said. "Those teenage girls careless enough to get pregnant go to Liverpool through the Brook Advisory Service... to a private clinic... but of course they cross charge us; it costs us a lot of money."

He seemed uncomfortable – but I wasn't sure whether he was embarrassed by his own lack of detailed knowledge or whether he was just uncomfortable talking about sex.

"STIs? Any particular cluster groups?" I asked. "There are probably huge seasonal variations, given the tourists along the coast?"

"You'd have to talk to the doctors in GUM," he said.

I wondered whether it was worth continuing down my list of questions... but I took one more stab before dismissing him as a waste of time and consigning the job specification that had excited me to the waste bin.

"What do you know about the sexual health needs of gay men in the area?"

"We don't have any of those here," he said, wringing his hands, his face flushed.

"No gay men... in Wrexham... in Prestatyn... really?"

"Homosexuality is not an issue for Welsh men."

I looked him in the eye, but he wouldn't hold my gaze.

"I don't know what to say to that. Homosexuality is clearly a reality for Welsh boys too, and frankly I'm finding it hard to believe that you've just said something so ridiculous."

He wrung his hands some more and didn't look at me. I thanked him for his time, and as I got up to leave I said,

"Are you really telling me that if I take this job I'll be the only gay man in north east Wales?" I was trying to provoke him but he didn't respond. I'd driven more than an hour for a meeting that was over in less than ten minutes and I felt disappointed that the job spec now seemed to be pie in the sky.

Back in Liverpool, Jupp and I had a long conversation. He persuaded me to attend the interview... he even persuaded me that working in such an apparently gay-hostile environment would be a challenge very different from the one in Liverpool.

I was offered the job.

I spent my first months as the new manager of the sexual health programme for north east Wales doing needs assessment work and met two amazing women – Dr Linda Egdell, who led the Family Planning Service and Dr Olwen Williams, the Consultant in Genito-Urinary Medicine. I persuaded my line manager that both these women should join him in forming an Advisory Group for the developmental phase of my work over the coming months. It was good to have them on board; neither needed any persuasion about the merits of Harm Reduction work and both, as senior doctors, had access and influence that I, as a non-medic, could never hope to realize... and they had contacts; I met a small group of single, teenage mothers, and many young gay men whose stories both saddened and inspired me. They also shared much anecdotal evidence about a group of largely middle aged men, mostly married, who met for sex in Tinkersdale... and the 'pretty police' who frequently tried to entrap them. It was in exploring more about the tales of Tinkersdale, in Hawarden Woods, that Dr Dafydd Alun Jones came briefly back into my life.

With the support of the newly appointed Director of Public Health, Dr Sandra Payne, a meeting was scheduled with senior police officers to discuss the policing of venues where men were meeting to have sex with other men. Sandra Payne had attended one of the meetings I held regularly with Olwen Williams and Linda Egdell and she was keen to see if the police would listen to the Harm Reduction arguments and agree to a less aggressive form of policing that might offer opportunities for health promotion and safer sex education.

On the appointed afternoon three senior police officers came to the Mold headquarters of the Public Health Department – accompanied by their 'medical adviser'. Sandra Payne opened the proceedings and made a clear and comprehensive case for a harm reduction approach to work with men who have sex with men in public places, citing examples of work done elsewhere in Britain (including my own team's work in Liverpool) where previously aggressive 'entrapment' policing had given way to a health promotion approach which in many cases reduced the incidence of such public behaviour as the men could be directed to more safe environments like saunas. Dr Dafydd Alun Jones had fidgeted throughout Dr Payne's presentation and when she sat down he began to tell of the 'rehabilitation work' he was doing with the men the police arrested. His narrative even included the account of an evening he had spent with a police officer in the roof space of a public toilet watching through a spy hole in the ceiling as the men below had sex with one another. The meeting ended abruptly when the most senior of the police officers said that they would not change their policing policy and would indeed continue to refer the arrested men to Dr D A Jones care. I had remained silent throughout the meeting... a silence which shames me to this day. Only with the arrival of a new Chief Constable in the late 1990s, and the tenure of Jack Straw as the Home Secretary in Blair's first government, did police attitudes towards gay men (and men who have sex with men) in north Wales begin to soften. I became the chair of the first LGB/Police liaison group in north Wales in 1999.

In the Clwyd Education Service I met Sylvia Jones, a Senior Education Officer with responsibility for teachers' in-service training. A radical, lesbian feminist, Sylvia had played a prominent role in the protests against the introduction of Section 28 of the Local Government Act in 1988 and was a staunch advocate of up-front and inclusive (of same sex issues) school based sex education. She was a breath of fresh air and after only a couple of meetings the potential for a work programme of teachers' training began to take shape. And Sylvia introduced me to her coven of radical lesbians, a 'cohort' whose health needs (including sexual health) was rarely considered.

As I came to know Linda Egdell, Olwen Williams, Sandra Payne and Sylvia Jones, I came to understand that each one of these remarkable women had networks that influenced public opinion in Wales – perhaps only in small ways – but influence never-the-less. With these four women in mind, juxtaposed with the nationally adopted intention of Health Promotion Wales to help build healthy public policy and create supportive environments in which individuals could choose healthier lifestyles and behaviours, I started to write short fiction about the lives of gay men in Wales – based on the stories I'd heard... stories that were largely unknown: And without stories people are closed in silence. My first collection of short fiction was published in 2000... its title: *Welsh Boys Too*. A slim volume, it won 'Honour Book' status in the 2002 American Library Association Stonewall Book Awards. A second, equally slim volume of stories, *Fishboys of Vernazza*, appeared in 2003, which was short-listed for the Welsh Book of the Year. *With Angels and Furies*, my first novel, followed in 2005, and on a snowy night in November 2008, a second novel *Crawling Through Thorns*, was launched in Denbigh Library, just a mile from the old asylum.

Writing. It's a strange gift to have offered a man who struggled to read.

15

WDR4 – Penny Lane

The Beatles wake us up, singing *Penny Lane*.

Colin Oxenforth had been patient with me. The congregation at St Margaret's on Princes Road was an interesting mix of post-riots Toxteth: elderly ladies in twin sets and pearls, black families, university students and some white professional types, most of whom were gay men. Under David Sheppard, the diocese had become a haven for gay priests, and whilst many hid behind their closet door, some were honest and 'discreet'... though Colin walked close to the edge of openness and was often seen in Scarlett's or Sadie's. I'd been a Reader for about a year when the whispering between the pews, that I'd make a good priest, caught my ear.

"But I live an openly gay life with Jupp," I said to Colin, who really didn't need to be told because he'd been to ours for dinner many times.

"But you don't rub your gayness into people's faces," Colin said.

"I think that's a matter of opinion... and of the gay

priests I know in this city, not one is living openly with another man."

"You might be surprised... couples can be inconspicuous without being deliberately deceptive."

"Okay... I understand enough about 'being called' to take what you're saying seriously, but —."

"Why don't you just go and have a chat with the Director of Ordinands?"

"I'm not jumping through hoops for the church and living a double life, Colin; Jupp is too important to me to hide him – and I won't deny that he's my partner... and I know how destructive living a lie can be – I've been there. If I am being called to the priesthood then it will be that 'priesthood of all believers'.

"Just go and talk to him for an hour... that won't commit you to anything and you may feel differently when you hear what he's got to say."

It wasn't so far from Penny Lane that I met the Director of Ordinands. The hoops he laid out before me – through which I would be expected to jump – were not hoops I was willing to negotiate.

"If I have to tell lies to be able to serve the church, then maybe the church isn't worth serving," I said.

"But what if your call is authentic," he asked.

"I don't have to lie to serve God."

Within a few months of starting the new job in Wales, in 1991, we moved out of Liverpool to live in Little Neston – just within the Cheshire border. The Bishop of Chester was known for his 'Biblical' understanding of homosexuality and he refused to endorse the transfer of my licence as a Reader to the parish church in Neston... and so, feeling worn down by the institutional homophobia of the church – and beginning to understand that I would never feel wholly accepted in the pews – my estrangement from 'church' began for a second time. Sundays became days for recreation – as well as re-creation: Jupp and I discovered that we liked walking... we walked from Liverpool's Pier Head along the canal to Leeds... we followed Wainwright's route from St Bee's Head to Robin Hood's Bay... we hiked the English-Welsh border along Offa's Dyke – and then continued around Wales along the coastal path.

I missed the rituals, the litany and the Eucharist... but I didn't miss them for long. Sometimes, if I had to work late, perhaps to attend a school governor's meeting in one of the coastal towns, I'd join in the Choral Evensong at the cathedral in St Asaph, and just once or twice a year – true to my Calvinistic roots – take communion. When asked if I'm 'religious' I say no... but my faith has never faltered and has matured with my greying hair.

16

Mordkommission Istanbul

We bought a television in the weeks after we arrived in Germany because we thought it would help me learn German. In that respect it has served its purpose. It's a 'smart tv' and we're able to access thousands of archived programmes from the main channels through the internet. Watching documentaries – often nature programmes or travel features, where the commentary is clear and a beat slower than the dialogue in dramas or talk shows – has brought on my listening skills and developed my passive understanding. Now I just need to speak more.

In Britain, before our telly blew up, we'd come home from work and sit in front of the box until late into the night – for some thirty hours a week! Realizing that we were both addicts, we decided not to replace the dead television and for almost three decades we lived without one. Jupp discovered Bridge (that's an addiction too), I started writing (another addiction?), we both read a lot and we became passionate listeners of Radio Four. Thirty years of television abstention, however, didn't free us from our compulsive viewing habit. I justify three or four hours in front of the flatscreen on the wall by convincing myself I'm learning the language... and I knit woollen socks (winters are so cold here) to further convince myself that I'm not wasting my time.

Mordkommission Istanbul is my favourite *Krimi*... Midsomer Murders in modern-day Istanbul – where everyone speaks German (ridiculous really!). Always in a crisp white shirt and smart dark suit, Inspector Mehmet Özakin, played by the Turkish-German actor Erol Sander (born Urçun Salihoğlu in Turkey but raised in Germany), is an urbane, heart-throb... and in every episode we get to see his bare chest. It's one of the few dramas I can follow – perhaps because one of the main viewing cohorts is the three million Turkish population here, so the dialogue is clear, moderately paced without sounding stilted, and less dialectal than in the many other gritty detective series that pad out the schedules.

In this week's episode, Inspector Özakin and his side-kick Mustafa Tombul (who is unlucky in love and wears silly bow ties) were investigating the murder of a young doctor. As the investigation progressed it became apparent that the dead doctor, haunted by a bad conscience, was about to spill the beans on a cash-for-kidneys racket at the private clinic where she worked... a clinic where rich Germans, who had to wait too long in Germany for a transplant, paid many tens of thousands of Euros for their life-saving operations whilst paying little heed to the peasants from Anatolia who were paid just a few thousand Turkish Lira (never more than €750) for their 'donation'.

And I thought of Dorothy Rowe.

She liked to be called Dots, which I never liked – but I liked her a lot. We became firm friends in the weeks after I arrived in Berkeley in 1981 and I often joked that if my gaydar was to malfunction, and I was to wake up one day a little more interested in women, that she would be my first choice.

Dorothy married a research scientist and he eventually went to work for a drug company; he made lots of money and her letters, these were pre-e-mail days, were filled with anecdotes about trips to Alaska and Peru (where her uncle, an archaeologist, had spent much of his working life at Machu Picchu), to Canada, Mexico and Hawaii. She and Gary didn't have children; her diabetes had affected her fertility. By the late 1990s, it had caused diabetic nephropathy; kidney disease. In one of her e-mails (no longer the beautifully handwritten letters on mauve watermarked note paper) she described the monotony of three four-hour sessions per week on the dialysis machine, and the seemingly interminable wait for a suitable kidney donor. She wrote how she sometimes found herself daydreaming that some wonderfully fit and healthy person would be fatally injured in a road traffic accident so that she might regain her life... and how, waking from such daydreams, she'd come out in a cold sweat realising what a nightmare she was wishing on some anonymous family.

I must have read Dorothy's e-mail half a dozen times over the next days. In response to my question about a suitable donor in her family she explained that they'd been down that route and reached a dead end – for medical reasons she didn't volunteer.

I don't think I consciously thought through a proposal to offer Dorothy one of my kidneys. However, sub-consciously I must have been weighing-up what I'd learnt from my studies in anatomy and physiology as part of my first degree in Biology: that we humans are born with an over-engineered kidney capacity and that with only a single kidney working at 75% of its maximal efficiency, human life is still very well sustained. And perhaps there was an element of mid-life crisis weaving through my sub-consciousness too: a gay man in my early forties... no kids... leaving no real impression on the world... leaving nothing behind. What was happening with Dorothy was important and I had the opportunity to make a real difference in her life.

It was one evening over supper that I said to Jupp, "I wonder if it's possible for me to donate a kidney to Dorothy?"

"Dorothy?" he quizzed. "Who's Dorothy?"

"Dorothy and Gary... we stayed with them in Seattle just before they moved to Philadelphia; you liked the view of Mount St Helen's from their lounge window."

Jupp laughed, which really put me off my stride, and said that the chances of a cross match were so remote that I should save myself the bother.

"If the chances are really so bad you won't mind if I make enquiries at the transplant centre in Liverpool," I said. "It might all be a non-starter, but at least I know I'll have tried."

"You're already a 'friend of Dorothy'," Jupp said with a shrug of his shoulders. "This is about as fat-fetched as the *Wizard of Oz*."

I spoke on the phone with the transplant co-ordinator at the Royal Liverpool Hospital. "Live, non-related donors aren't that common in Britain," she said, "but it does happen. I'll put some information in the post for you."

"Should I say anything yet... to my friend in the States?"

"No. You really mustn't raise her hopes before we even know whether you're a suitable donor. Do you know if you're even the same blood group?"

"I've no idea."

"Okay – I'll send you the donor information pack that we've put together and when you've read it, if you're still keen to move things on, you could come in and have a chat."

From my first visit to the Renal Unit on the top floor of the Royal Liverpool Hospital in early March 1999, to the day of our departure for the United States, some ten months elapsed. Twenty years on, the sequence of events during that time is blurred. An internet search (as I write) brought back some memories of the stepped process – lots of blood tests... collecting urine over two twenty-four hour periods... frequent blood pressure measurements (just once my diastolic pressure – the bottom number – was in the nineties but the Consultant Nephrologist didn't seem overly concerned)... counselling sessions to judge my competence and my motives... an intravenous pyelogram (IVP) – an x-ray procedure where dye is injected into the blood to visualize any abnormalities in the urinary system, including the kidneys and bladder... a renal angiogram – which meant a day in the hospital, where the artery in the groin was punctured with a needle, and a fine tube (cannula) passed up into the artery. Once the tip of the cannula was in position close to the kidneys, injected dye gave a clear picture of the arterial structure of each kidney. Apparently it's not uncommon to have more than one artery feeding a kidney and in such cases surgery to remove the kidney becomes more complicated.

Jupp also had to agree to be interviewed. Because of the stepped nature of the 'selection' process, he became resigned to my decision and agreed not to offer any objections. And as the weeks passed, and the possibility that I would donate a kidney became more likely, he was nothing but wholly supportive of me. "A person willing to give a kidney to a friend is a pretty special kind of person and it's made me love you even more," he said one day. "But I still think you're off your head!"

By December, amid all the frenzy about the Millennium Bug that might send everyone's computers into apoplexy, the hospital in Philadelphia confirmed that they were satisfied with all the data they had received from Liverpool and someone from the Department of Health in London had agreed that I, as a British citizen, could travel to the US to donate a kidney to an American citizen, and the dates for the surgery were set for the second week in January 2000. It was time to tell my parents.

Neither Megan nor Terry could remember meeting Dorothy when they had visited me in California (to be fair, they met a lot of people on that trip). Megan seemed both anxious and proud in equal measure. Terry couldn't understand why I'd put my own life at risk for a virtual stranger... and wasn't I an AIDS risk? I wanted to tell him that many gay men who'd experienced hostility and rejection from members of their birth family often chose a new 'family' to 'be there' for them, and that far from being a 'virtual stranger', Dorothy was my 'sister' – but I self-censored... swallowed my words... and let his disapproval go.

My work gave me a three-month paid special leave and as the news got around people stopped me in the corridors and in the canteen to say how brave... selfless... virtuous... and just plain stupidly wonderful I was. "You'd do the same for someone you loved," I'd fire back at them... and sometimes you could see in their faces that they wouldn't.

We flew first class. I'd tried to explain over the telephone to Dorothy's mother that we didn't expect any favours or financial gain but she said it was the least she could do to honour my gift to her.

The surgeon came around a couple of hours after I'd been admitted. He was younger than I'd expected. He talked with Jupp and me for a while, referring back to the notes he'd been sent from the Royal Liverpool Hospital. Then he did a quick physical examination and took my blood pressure.

"You're a bit anxious I expect," he said as he noted the numbers on my chart. He scanned the notes from Liverpool again. "There's no history of high blood pressure in your family is there?" With some puzzlement I said that there wasn't, as far as I knew.

Over the next couple of hours my blood pressure continued to rise and by the middle of the afternoon it seemed to level off at 180 over 120... and that's where it hovered for the three days that I stayed in the hospital.

I was depressed for many weeks after my attempt to donate was aborted by Dorothy's medical team. Of course, Dorothy and Gary (and her mother who'd paid for our first-class tickets) were distraught – to have come so close,

only to have all their hopes thwarted – but they were so
gracious with me. Jupp was wonderfully tender and kept
assuring me that despite the thoughts in my head and the
desires of my heart, my body finally said a very definite
no... and that everything was alright. I became
preoccupied with notions of failure and for the first time
in my life I questioned whether it was indeed better to
have tried and failed than not to have tried at all. Just
days after arriving home my blood pressure settled back
down at 110 over 70 and I went back to work. Routine
carried me for quite some time before I regained my
equilibrium.

A couple of weeks after we returned home I received a
card from Dorothy:
*You must think about what you have given to me and Gary,
and not think about what couldn't in the end be given. I've
grown used to being let down by my body over the years.
Count yourself lucky that the way in which your body let us
all down hasn't caused you any long-term physical harm. I
know that you're upset, but please know and understand
that the gifts you gave me this past year are priceless. You
renewed my faith in the depth and breadth of friendship,
you restored my trust in loyalty, you showed us kindness the
like of which is never forgotten... and most of all you gave
me something to hope for.*

Dorothy received a kidney from another seminary friend (who'd been inspired by the story of my offer) in the autumn of 2000, and she and Gary visited us in Neston the following summer. It was wonderful to see her so full of energy and enjoying a new lease of life. Sadly, a stroke, brought on by complications from her diabetes, cut her life short and she died in December 2016.

17

Dros y Dŵr

Another social media memory jog! *Fifteen gay men and a lesbian for afternoon tea; scones and cream, apple and almond cake, Bara Brith and lemon drizzle. Is Barmouth ready for the pink invasion?*

We bought Dros y Dŵr in 2010. Described by the Barmouth estate agent as an 'imposing, immaculate, double-fronted, four storey Victorian Villa', we both knew, from the first recce, that we would make it a comfortable home... and get paying guests to fund the astronomical heating bills! In an elevated position above the iconic railway viaduct crossing the Mawddach, the views from the front terrace and the bay windows on the ground and first floors could take your breath away. Twice a day the estuary ebbed and flowed, the ever-changing vista a contrast to the solid majesty of Cadair Idris across the water. The couple selling the house had spent many tens of thousands renovating and modernising; "It provides a steady income," he said as he showed us around, "but the only way to make a small fortune from a B&B in Barmouth is to come here with a large fortune, especially with these beautiful old houses – they need a lot of TLC... of course, we've got all the guarantees from the re-roofing, the re-wiring, the new plumbing and central heating system." They'd only been in the house six years... but they'd been unlucky in health, so they were moving on.

We opened the door to guests for the first time at Easter, after a frantic six weeks of redecorating and replacing three slightly grubby-looking carpets. It was a gloriously sunny weekend and Barmouth glistened. With only three guest bedrooms, and just six guests, we were still classed as a private house (which freed us from a raft of regulations and local business taxes), and the workload was manageable without the hassle of having to take on casual staff. During that first weekend we made three decisions which made our lives as B&B hosts a little less stressful: there would be no more croissants served at breakfast – just look at the mess they make; greasy flakes all over the floor! We'd take no children under 12 – just look at the mess they make, especially when their parents take no responsibility for eggy fingers on the paintwork in the newly decorated dining room... and there'd be a two-night minimum stay – because who wants to wash and iron sheets after just one night? We'd already made the choice not to live behind locked doors, and though all the guest rooms had locks, our living space at the top of the house was open to anyone who wandered up that far – not that anyone ever did in seven years. And there were to be no televisions in the rooms! Hadn't we both, in our past professional lives, stayed in hotels and guest houses where we'd been woken by a neighbouring guest's lonely passion for the porn channel at two in the morning? When we registered with one of the best known holiday accommodation websites we had a long discussion with them about openly advertising the fact that we were TV and child free. Their representative was sceptical, but these two features became hugely popular reasons why our guests came to us, and kept coming back to us – though the home-made breads, cakes, jams and marmalades, and a generous breakfast may have had something to do with it too. For three years we were the top rated B&B in Barmouth. For ten months of the year we were able to fill our rooms (making a respectable living) and over seven years we received visitors form fifty-six nations... the world coming to us.

Sadly, the guests that caused us hassle (in one way or another) are the ones we mostly remember: the lah-di-dah home-counties couple who were so up their own backsides they'd forgotten how to smile, or say *hello* or *thank-you* – they stayed for a week and their bad attitude drained us both... and that Welsh-speaking hippie couple from Anglesey who smoked pot in bed – in their 'heightened state of chill', they scorched the cotton sheets and spilled coffee on the brand new carpet... and that fundamentalist-evangelical Christian couple, Bibles on each bedside table, who left abruptly when they realised we were a gay couple… and the terminally ill woman who overdosed on her morphine pain relief.

We do also remember some of the folk whose holiday spirit led to sexual abandon; those anecdotes continue to evoke ripples of laughter at dinner parties: The gay couple whose athletic approach to intercourse caused the brass chandelier in the guest lounge beneath them to swing precariously – and break the slats under the mattress of their bed; the Polish couple who, from the sound of their shrieks and sighs, enjoyed a dozen or more orgasms during a three day spell of torrential rain that caused extensive flooding along the estuary. Their lusty exuberance embarrassed us and our other guests, but fortunately we could all see the funny side of it, and what else was one to do in such abysmal weather? And then, what about the two police officers from a Midlands police force? They were (apparently) at a conference in Llandudno; they texted their respective spouses between their love-making – and he forgot to remove his used condoms from under the bed before they left in separate cars. Servicing their room after they'd gone, I recall reflecting that it was a very long time since I'd had a 'three condom night'. Oh… yes… and the cock rings! A guy left his varied collection in a beautifully embossed leather toilet bag on the bathroom shelf – and wanted them returned by post: "But don't bother sending the leather bag," he said over the phone.

"That will cost too much. Just put my rings in a padded envelope." He'd said nothing on the phone about the purple silicone anal plug or the vibrating prostate massager we also found in the bag. And there was that somewhat timid, middle-aged couple from Lincoln; after they'd left, Jupp discovered three 'abused' chocolate croissants in their bed. We were never sure if it was a fetish they shared, or if they were just messy, quirky eaters. Chocolate stains are really hard to remove from white cotton sheets!

Most of our guest were lovely people – and some of the loveliest were the 'beer gut and tattoo brigade' that often descend on Barmouth on bank-holiday weekends; many of these tattooed women were warm and funny, considerate and respectful, and really challenged our prejudices and preconceived ideas. And a lot of our guests were naturists; the only official 'clothing optional' beach in Wales is just a couple of miles north of Barmouth, drawing sun-loving nudists from all over the country. Just once a couple asked if they could come down for breakfast nude – a request we felt we had to decline despite being regular visitors to the beach ourselves.

Baking was just something I'd always been able to do and there was always a selection of home-made cakes for guests when they arrived (usually) mid-afternoon, but afternoon teas became grander, more regular events after we were contacted, within weeks of opening, by the Gay Outdoor

Club (GOC) – a nation-wide rambling association of queer folk that we had often walked with when we'd lived in Liverpool. GOC teas were always pre-arranged events – usually on a Saturday or a Sunday – and cakes and scones for ten, fifteen, twenty sometimes rain-drenched hikers was not uncommon. We decided that we couldn't charge for afternoon tea! Charging per head would be problematic in a small seaside town with a dozen cafes each trying to make a living... but donations to the Barmouth lifeboat were suggested and a suitably large earthenware pot was placed on the windowsill.

Ann Thomas, a friend from Dolgellau who worked for the Snowdonia National Park then contacted us; could we provide afternoon tea for visiting groups of Germans and Austrians who came to stay at the park's study centre, Plas Tan y Bwlch, in Maentwrog, through a Berlin based travel agency, *Boundless. Kaffee und Kuchen* on our terrace at the end of their hike along the Mawddach Trail would be ideal... for through Ann's eyes, as the hike leader, keeping the group together at the end of the day was important – losing members of her party in the warren of paths in Old Barmouth was her worst nightmare when she needed to get them all back on the minibus. And so the large earthenware pot found its place on the windowsill again – and again. Over the years, between GOC and the *Boundless* adventurers, hundreds of pounds found their way into the local lifeboat station fund.

Afternoon tea at Dros y Dŵr – and especially the home-made scones and lemon drizzle, became a talking point in the Berlin offices of *Boundless* after much positive feedback on their website. Through Ann Thomas, and after a phone call from the Berlin bureau, Jupp was offered work as an interpreter/translator for some six to eight weeks a year; the *Boundless* tours in the Snowdonia National Park were 'a walking and cultural tour with lectures and heritage experiences', all of which required simultaneous translation. Jupp loved these adventures and after three or four years, when Ann retired, Jupp sometimes led the groups himself. Meanwhile, I found managing the comings and goings at Dros y Dŵr single-handed stressful and exhausting, and in warm weather, when my dicky heart seemed to slow me down, I disliked running the show alone.

With all our rooms occupied and no arrivals or departures, we could usually finish the daily chores – preparing and serving breakfast, the clean-up, starting off the bread (to be baked later in the day), servicing the guests' rooms, vacuuming the hall, stairs and landing and the daily shop for fresh produce – by lunchtime. On such days, I could visit my mother in the care home, and even go to the beach in the afternoon or walk in the hills behind the town – always with the dogs – as there was no pressure to be back before 4pm to welcome new guests. However, departure and arrival days were much busier; depending on how messy the guests had been, turning a room around could take an hour or... much longer: cleaning mud, coffee and red wine stains off carpets, curtains and/or walls (which was not uncommon) could take an age and if our guests were very hairy or the men had a poor aim then cleaning the bathrooms could be nightmarish – chasing pubic hairs around the shower cubicles is arduous! On such days we may both put in seven or eight hours work... so on a *Boundless* week, when 'holding the fort' alone, I could work a fifteen hour day... and the dogs would look doe-eyed because they hadn't had their usual walk!

It was on such a *Boundless* week I discovered that the dogs loved to chase the trains across the 700 meter viaduct below the house. Just after six one morning – an hour before I needed to be in the kitchen preparing breakfast – I'd taken Wash and Nel to the small beach beneath the north end of the bridge, just minutes from the house. To the south, across the wide estuary mouth, the railway line rises from Fairbourne and hugs the cliff on its route towards Shrewsbury. In the quiet of the morning the dogs heard the early train's whistle as it left Fairbourne for Barmouth. And off they went along the walkway (separated from the tracks by a high wooden fence)... seven hundred meters to meet the train at the far end of the bridge – and then a mad dash back. Chasing the early morning and late night trains (when few pedestrians were crossing the bridge) became their sport and many of the train drives would lean from their window and call them on. We even found video clips on social media, taken by train drivers, of Wash and Nel's race across the Mawddach!

Barmouth has just two and a half thousand residents, so my return to my hometown didn't escape notice. Within weeks of our arrival, whilst browsing in the art gallery next door to the chapel where I'd been baptized, I overheard the owner, Valerie McArdell and her co-worker, Sue Slater discussing the need for new blood on the town council. A few weeks before, when Jupp and I had bought a couple of prints at the gallery for the dining room at Dros y Dŵr, both women had been interested in our story and my return to my roots. Admiring a small, original water colour of Barmouth harbour, and wondering about the wisdom of placing an original costing a few hundred pounds in our guests' lounge, my thoughts were interrupted.

"Would you be interested in serving on the town council," Valerie asked.

"No... no interest at all," I said. "Can you put 'maybe sold' on this one and I'll ask Jupp to come in and see if he likes it?"

Before the local government reorganisation of 1974, Barmouth had an urban district council which ran the local services, and a mayor who wore a gold chain at many a civic event. I remembered from my childhood that the mayor (and his wife the mayoress – for the mayor was always a man in those days) walked in the annual Remembrance Day parade behind the town's silver band (in which my father played the trombone) to the cenotaph in the park, where he laid a wreath on behalf of the community. Barmouth, then, had much civic pride. In 1963, Mr Iorwerth Richards, one of the Elders from our chapel was the mayor. As a seven-year-old, holding my mother's hand so as not to get lost in the crowd, I watched Mr Richards welcome the Queen (the one and only time I ever saw her) as she stepped from the Royal Train in Barmouth station, his gold chain glinting in the August sunshine. Then in 1965, Mr L E Jones, another Elder from Park Road chapel who served as the town's mayor (his wife always in a fur coat and grand hat), welcomed our retired headmaster and my Sunday school teacher, W D Williams, home from the National Eisteddfod in Newtown where he'd been that year's chaired bard – a civic reception like few could remember. And in 1966, Mayor Trefor Williams and his wife, the novelist Eirlys Trefor, looked so glamorous in an open topped Hillman Minx at the front of the carnival parade.

But after 1974, when Barmouth became officially Abermaw under the new Gwynedd administration and its services were run from Dolgellau, the town seemed to lose some of the sense of itself... and the town council, so it seemed through my adolescent eyes, only concerned itself with sand, blown into the streets and sometimes blocking the promenade, and dog shit. I'm somewhat embarrassed to acknowledge that on my return to Barmouth all those years later, my understanding of the role and function of a small community council hadn't matured.

Sue Slater and Valerie McArdell persisted over many weeks; whenever I passed the gallery, if they had no customers, they'd beckon me inside... and almost without realizing, I came to understand a little more about the role and function of the town council. I was co-opted onto Barmouth Town Council in 2012, there being insufficient interest in the community to mount an election to fill the vacant seat.

Committee work wasn't new to me, though I was sometimes exasperated by how long the chair would allow for the discussion of what seemed quite straightforward issues... our monthly meetings lasting up to three hours when an hour would have sufficed. Little wonder there was such apathy amongst the community for participation in local democracy. After a brief piece in the local newspaper, the *Cambrian News*, introducing Councillor John Sam Jones to the local community – with no mention of my being gay or my marriage to Jupp, which surprised us both; had rural Wales really embraced homosexuality? – I was stopped regularly on my walks with the dogs by local people... concerned about the damage to the sea defences at the end of the promenade after the previous winter's storms... troubled by the fishermen peeing off Barmouth bridge... furious about the dog shit on the footpaths in the parkland near the football pitch... annoyed that the narrow pavements were obstructed during the holiday season with the clutter of street furniture and advertising A-boards... pissed off with fly tipping... upset about a planning application that would inevitably obscure a view of the sea or the mountains... cheesed-off with the drunken behaviour of teenagers in the park overlooking the harbour... insufficient litter bin collections – the detritus from the town's four fish and chip shops littering the streets and promenade... blown sand... aggressive seagulls... and children being 'forced' to speak Welsh in the local schools. Some issues were easily dealt with locally – though I was unsuccessful in my efforts to persuade the chip shop owners to opt for recyclable chip trays... polystyrene kept the food warm! Those matters that fell under the responsibility of the county council, though duly reported to the appropriate department, were often ignored... and I came to understand the disillusionment of many local people with Gwynedd County Council. There was, of course, an expectation that each town councillor would take a 'seat' on one or two of the many active community groups. I was co-opted on to the governing body of the local primary school, Ysgol y Traeth, serving as a school governor for four years – and as chair of the governors for a year.

I was a popular town councillor, amongst both the local community and my fellow councillors, and in May 2014 I became the chair of the town council (no meeting I chaired ever lasting longer than 90 minutes!) and mayor of Barmouth. In a short address before the council voted on my nomination I did ask whether Barmouth was ready for an openly gay mayor – I didn't want to become the news and detract from the mayor's role and tasks. My question was dismissed with a wave of the hand and again, even the *Cambrian News* didn't consider my sexual orientation worthy of mention – the fact that I was a Welsh-speaking local boy seemed more newsworthy. Not even when Jupp wore the *Mayoress' Chain* as my consort at civic events did the local press make a fuss. (I should explain that the *Mayoress' Chain* had been re-polished by one of the female mayors who had preceded me, erasing the word 'mayoress' engraved on the central shield, so that her husband could wear it). However, his presence at my side did cause some confusion on the grand occasion of the start of the Three Peaks Yacht Race (from Barmouth to Fort William). One of the many spectators mistook Jupp for a visiting German *Bürgermeister* from a twin town. Jupp explained that he was the Mayor's husband. "My God – is Barmouth so modern?" came the response. "Indeed it is," he said.

Jupp and I often reflected on the genuine warmth of the welcome we received in Barmouth as an openly gay couple, but having lived our lives with the constant awareness of the menace of homophobia – and very occasionally feeling the barbs of its scorn – we sometimes pinched ourselves, wondering if we were truly accepted or merely tolerated. Of one thing we were sure, however; the intolerance that had led to the efforts to cure me of being gay in the old asylum in Denbigh during the 1970s was no longer part of the zeitgeist.

Barmouth's Mayoral Chain of Office is an enduring symbol of continuity, of local identity and of civic pride. It's made of gold plated sterling silver and consists of three rows of shields (or wreaths), each engraved with the name of a previous mayor, and a larger, central ornately enamelled Council logo. It's worn over the shoulders and it's very heavy... and for me it was weighty with significance. There were the names of Iorwerth Richards, L E Jones, Trefor Williams – and mayors from the decades before I was born, and in the wearing of it I felt both humbled and empowered to represent the town that had been my family's home for almost three centuries.

I resigned my seat on the town council in the months after my mayoralty ended. Some of my fellow councillors, to this day, would say that I had a fit of pique! I struggled with what I could see, through the tint in my glasses, as an inconsistency in the way we as a council addressed failures in compliance with local licencing laws; sometimes we'd come down like a ton of bricks and at other times we'd pussy-foot. After challenging one of the instances where we'd trodden ever so softly so as not to cause 'upset', my challenge was dismissed by my colleagues – so I walked.

Some good came from my resignation. A number of young people, who'd followed my 'Mayor's Page' on social media, put their names forward for the vacant seat and there was an election for the town council for the first time in more than a decade.

18

Heimat

It's April (2020) and we've been in Germany for three years. We still speak English with one another; we're both such different people in German... Jupp is less relaxed, less patient, and perhaps a bit less considerate (and certainly a more aggressive driver) – almost as though he's reconnected with some pre-British version of himself or has breathed in too much toxic German maleness. My spoken German is broken – and though I can now 'get-by', I'm less confident, less willing to share an opinion, less exuberant – so my Germanic self is not someone I'm growing to like... not yet, anyway! It's chicken and egg, of course; the more fluent I become the more I will perhaps like my new identity, but even on the days we begin speaking German over breakfast we usually slip into English by coffee time. It is fascinating how language defines so much about who we understand ourselves to be... and how relationships are so grounded in forms of speech.

As the husband of a German national I became eligible for naturalisation on April Fool's Day. Of course, the process costs hundreds of Euros and I have to take two tests – the *Einbürgerungstest*, with questions about German culture, politics, history and geography, and a German language test. As a consequence, I'm more focussed in my efforts to embrace the language and culture of my new homeland.

It was Boris Johnson's decisive victory in the December 2019 election that sealed my determination to re-gain my European Union citizenship by becoming a German citizen. It was Johnson's victory, too, that quelled some of the anger I was still harbouring about the British people's decision to leave the EU. In a reflective mood, in the last days of December, I was reading about Nelson Mandela and pondered his thoughts as he was about to be released from years of incarceration: "As I stand before the door to my freedom I realise that if I do not leave my pain, anger and bitterness behind me, I will still be in prison." Of course, I'm not in prison... I live a comfortable and blessed life in Germany, but as the year and the decade changed there was a metaphorical door which beckoned. Like Mandela, I too understood that carrying anger, hurt and bitterness with me into the future would be self-limiting. It was time, then, to let go of my Brexit Blues. I wouldn't continue to let the holding of this grudge make me bitter – so I released it... I wouldn't continue to allow the clench of anger to sour my spirit – so I released it... I wouldn't any longer nurture the sense of betrayal that caused an ache in my heart... even though I wasn't sure, and I'm still not sure what it means yet to forgive a nation's folly.

We woke up on Saturday the first of February to Mary Hopkin singing *Those were the days*. The United Kingdom had left the European Union and indeed, *nothing seemed the way it used to be*. In warm, winter sunshine (the mildest winter for many years according to the weather forecasters) we cycled for three hours on a route that criss-crosses the German/Dutch border, historically a relatively recent line on a map. This blood-soaked land, through the forest of the Meinweg, is peaceful today thanks to the battle weariness, the treaties, the vision and the new friendships that have forged the European Union.

The next day we hiked with Klaus, Marion and Marita, along the river Niers between Wankum and Wachtendonk. Close to the Benedictine monastery of Mariendonk, we pass an Eighteenth century standing stone marking the border between what were the lands of the Archbishop of Cologne and the Dukedom of Geldern in the days before the relatively recent concept of today's Germany was conceived. Today's border with the Netherlands is a few kilometres west. Outside the monastery, Marita, Marion and I sang *Hail Holy Queen*; we three sing in a gospel choir, the Joyful Voices of Niederkrüchten, and this spring we're working on songs from *Sister Act* in readiness for two summer concerts. I never thought of myself as a gospel singer; the theology is often more saccharine than I can stomach, but we have great fun in the Tuesday evening rehearsals.

We break the hike and eat lunch in the yard of a farm shop and restaurant, the unseasonal spring-like sunshine warm and the tubs of snowdrops cheery... and the largest schnitzel I've ever had is served up with very good chips – yes, here too the XXL portions contribute to obesity. Klaus wants to know if I'm ever home-sick. We have a conversation about the meaning of 'home'. Klaus, who's in his late fifties and married with an adult son and an infant grandchild, still thinks of the home where he grew up as 'home'. His mother is still alive and his brother still lives in the house where they were raised... "Where I live with Marion is 'our house' and I don't really think of it as home." He's surprised that I'm not pining for Barmouth, or Wales, or the United Kingdom. By now Effeld feels like home... is my home. Effeld, with its sterile stone gardens, the alpacas and kangaroos, its Saturday morning kneeling moss pickers and its dog poo, its fields of white gold, its lake... and my husband's family – and my husband... there is some truth in the hackneyed saying 'home is where the heart is'. Of course, there are people in Wales that I miss – indeed there are people from the California and Liverpool years too – but social media and the various visual communication apps available today bring these people into my home; if I'm honest, I 'see' and speak with my brother more now than before we moved to Germany and I talk regularly with friends in Dolgellau, Dyffryn Ardudwy, Washington D C and California.

That evening, after our hike, our neighbours, Jörg and Sabine – with their son Aaron – come to play board games, and when Aaron gets tired of losing and goes home to his computer games, the four of us play cards until late into the night. Contract Whist and Dirty Liz (or Black Lady – though Sabine calls the game Black Mamba) have become favourites with her and Jörg and we play at least once a week, so I've mastered numbers in German and learned many expletives. We're so lucky in our neighbours. They love our dogs, and Nel seems to have a love affair with Sabine that she's never had with Jupp or me. They are always eager to care for Wash and Nel if we go away. Aaron, who is thirteen now, comes to ours every Monday evening when Jupp is playing Bridge in the Netherlands and we speak English for an hour. His English is fast becoming better than my German.

In the days after my suicide attempt, forty-five years ago, it was Mair Wynne Griffith who said to me, "The journey is home, and sometimes, when it's uncomfortable or when we're feeling lost, we need company on that journey." It took me a while to understand home as a journey. Much of that journey has been at the edge of society – sometimes even at the edge of lost, but just as Mair sat with me for many hours over many days in the late winter of 1975, so I've had the company of many – not all named here because the list is too long – for more than half a lifetime. And I've had Jupp: He's kept me grounded... he's kept me from despair when the chasm at the edge seemed too wide. Being loved by him has given me strength, and loving him has given me courage.

So, it's the view from the edge that has been my home... that is my home... that will be my home. Today we're enjoying that view in Effeld. Tomorrow, or some other tomorrow – who knows? For as Mair said, "The journey is home."

Queer Square Mile

Queer Short Stories from Wales

Edited by
Kirsti Bohata,
Mihangel Morgan
and Huw Osborne

"It's so timely just to have so many of these stories pulled
together in one place... this really nails it..."
Dr Michelle Deininger

"Really well edited, really well introduced."
Charles Williams, BBC Wales Arts Review

"*Queer Square Mile* successfully anthologises
a queer Welsh canon."
Joshua Jones, Wales Arts Review

Isaac Romanov talks with **John Sam Jones** about his memoir, *The Journey Is Home: Notes from a Life on the Edge.* Published in both English and Welsh, The memoir *tells stories from throughout Jones' life as he journeyed from a boy on the Welsh coast to a scholar at Berkeley.*

I'd like to share a secret with you — I fall in love with titles. Not titles such as The Duke of here or The Screaming Queen of there, but titles of books (and films) — but not easily — so when I saw John Sam Jones' new release, *The Journey Is Home,* I fell in love with it. Not only did I fall for the title, but it made me think: often we are on our own journey, looking to the end (or planning a diversion), forgetting that wherever we are we should feel 'home' — be in the present, the here and now. John's title made me think about my life and my own journey, and then I was asked to do a Q&A with that same author — how lucky is that?

Isaac Romanov: I know you're in your sixties, John, and that a few years ago you had a serious heart scare, but that didn't seem to urge you to release a memoir then — why now? Did something happen to compel you to write it at this time?

John Sam Jones: My first 'heart scare' was in 2003 and during many weeks of convalescence I wrote a draft my second novel, *Crawling Through Thorns,* which was eventually published by Parthian in 2008. In the autumn of 2017 I had further cardiac problems and this did indeed spur me on to write the memoir Richard Davies at Parthian had been urging me to write. After some procrastination I began to work on *The Journey is Home* in 2018. It took almost a year to write, and after leaving it for some months to mature on the shelf the manuscript was eventually submitted in June 2019. COVID then delayed the process that led to its eventual publication in May 2021. Writing books, and getting them published, can be a long, long process.

Isaac Romanov: It makes complete sense to me that you, as a writer celebrated for their short stories, should write stories from your life rather than an autobiography, but were there any other reasons you chose a memoir approach?

John Sam Jones: I can write long! I've written two reasonably successful novels — one very long one that some would say was too long — but yes, you're right, I have been lauded for my short stories. I like the focus on the ordinariness of everyday life (of extraordinary people) which can take a central role in the short story, and on the significance underlying what is apparently trivial. The result of such writing can be really perceptive, revealing the subtleties of the human mind and of human behaviour.

To be honest, my thoughts about *autobiography* and *memoir* were confused. *Crawling Through Thorns* was an autobiographical novel, in that I took significant episodes from my own life, gave them to a fictitious character and built a fictitious world around him... and because in some respects I had told those aspects of the story of my life I wanted to tell in that novel, I wasn't sure what else there was to tell. Then I came across this description of memoir: 'it isn't the summary of a life; it's a window into a life...'. I began to think about different windows — faith, sexuality, family, secrets, electricity... — and this became a really appealing idea: a collection of writings exploring these themes that didn't have to follow the linear structure of 'the story of a life'.

Isaac Romanov: It seems to me you've spent a great deal of time caring for others (at times when it must have been extremely painful) — did you recognise this gift in the young John Sam Jones or did it evolve and flower over the years and through circumstances?

John Sam Jones: As a small child I loved our neighbour's cat, Sooty, who'd sometimes sit in my lap (whilst I sat on the doorstep because Sooty wasn't allowed into our house). And because we were not allowed to have a cat or a dog of our own, I finally persuaded my parents to let me have a rabbit. That rabbit, Bobby, was so *cwtched* and pampered! Yes, I suppose I seemed to be a gentle, caring sort of child.

Growing into my early teens the bullying began. It may be paradoxical, but one response to being bullied is to want to care more for people... because you don't want them to experience the loneliness and isolation and even the self-hatred that being the victim of bullying can induce.

Later, after Electric Shock Aversion Therapy and attempted suicide, Henri J M Nouwen's book *The Wounded Healer* had a profound influence on me, enabling me to understand how woundedness can become the source of compassion.

Isaac Romanov: In your first days in graduate school in Berkeley you were publicly *outed* to the entire school by the Dean of Students. That seems to have empowered and released you — can you say some more about that?

John Sam Jones: I went to Berkeley to study pastoral theology under the World Council of Churches (WCC) scholarship programme, and my specific area of interest (which had secured me the scholarship) was the response of churches in the San Francisco Bay Area to gay men and lesbians. Theological research and thinking in Berkeley is quite 'cutting edge' so it was one of the most exciting places in the western world to go, especially to explore the theology of sexuality. As the WCC Scholar for 1981–82, studying in this 'controversial' field, I was perceived as a bit of a 'trail blazer' I suppose, and the Dean of Students at Pacific School of Religion just hadn't thought that introducing this *gay man from Wales* was in any way unwise or unacceptable in the progressive, heady atmosphere of the Bay Area. Her outing of me was certainly empowering and I decided, more or less on the spot, that *John Sam Jones — gay man* was destined to be dealt with... which wasn't difficult to realise in and around San Francisco, but wasn't so easy or straightforward when I returned to the UK in 1984!

Isaac Romanov: After the traumatic experience of Electric Shock Aversion Therapy at the old asylum in Denbigh in 1975 you tried to take your own life. Fortunately you had two guardian angels, Huw and Mair Wynne Griffith. Their wisdom, patience and presence were a great help to you in rebuilding your life. Nearly fifty years on from then, do you believe there's still a need for guardian angels?

John Sam Jones: Don't we all need wise, patient mentors who will walk beside us when things get tough? Huw was a clergyman, and he was instrumental in helping me interpret those bits of scripture that, through one set of tinted glasses, can be read as condemning of homosexuality — and which had left me feeling wretched and beyond God's love. Interpretation of scripture is fundamental to understanding the themes those ancient stories are trying to illuminate, and over many weeks, Huw and I, through our study, did re-interpret those verses and came to a less malevolent understanding. And Mair? She sat with me through hours, through days of despair, 'because the journey is home and often we need company on the journey'.

Isaac Romanov: You've worn several hats during your varied career — all of them have been important and influential in their own way, but do you have one that gave you a feeling of complete achievement and fulfilment more than the others?

John Sam Jones: In real time it's often not possible to get any sense of achievement beyond the fulfilment of very specific goals. I understood the depth of the privilege that it was to sit alongside a murderer in Walton Prison and recite a beloved Psalm together. I was humbled to hold the hand of many young men, abandoned by their family, as AIDS wreaked its havoc. I was heartened to discover recently (listening to the ex-director of Public Health for Mersey Region on the radio) that the HIV prevention work I was involved with in Liverpool in the mid/late 1980s had a significant impact in limiting the long-term spread of HIV in that city.

But I think to give an honest answer to your question, I'd have to say that it is the responses to my writing! Receiving a letter saying that reading *Crawling Through Thorns* had saved a life... Being approached by a man from the audience after a reading at a literature festival who said that my short stories had helped him understand his son... I believe that 'giving voice to the voiceless' through my stories is reward enough for trying to live as the best gay man I can be.

Isaac Romanov: *The Journey is Home* is published in Welsh and English and the Welsh-language version, translated by Sian Northey under the title *Y Daith ydi Adra*, is your first book to be released in Welsh — how does this make you feel?

John Sam Jones: I'm absolutely delighted. Bilingualism is a strange attribute... It's frustrating to me, as a fluent Welsh speaker, that I never discovered the gift of writing prose in Welsh (I do write letters and emails). Sian's translation is outstanding and the significance of having a gay themed memoir in the Welsh language can't be over-stated. I read novels in both Welsh and English, but in talking with Sian I discovered that there are Welsh speakers in Wales who read very little in English, so I'm very happy that they have the opportunity to read this memoir in their chosen language.

Isaac Romanov: Is this memoir complete, or is it a first instalment? Should we be on the lookout for a part two further down the line?

John Sam Jones: Is a memoir ever a complete appraisal? There were stories I had to leave untold because to have shared them would have outed men whom I have no right to out, and there were stories omitted because those involved said they'd rather not see their names in print... but some other tomorrow life will have moved on and I will see the world through a different set of glasses, so things that seemed insignificant when I was writing *The Journey is Home* may perhaps have taken on new meanings.

This interview was first published in the *Wales Arts Review*, reprinted with kind permission.

Isaac Romanov has worked in many areas over the years including public education and research. He lives with his husband Ian in the hamlet of Bethlehem, Carmarthenshire.

PARTHIAN   Fiction

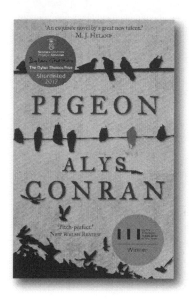

Pigeon

ALYS CONRAN
ISBN 978-1-910901-23-6
£8.99 • Paperback

**Winner of Wales
Book of the Year**

'An exquisite novel by a great
new talent.' – M.J. Hyland

Ironopolis

GLEN JAMES BROWN
ISBN 978-1-912681-09-9
£10.99 • Paperback

**Shortlisted for the Orwell
Award for Political Fiction and
the Portico Prize**

'A triumph' – *The Guardian*

'The most accomplished
working-class novel of the
last few years.' – *Morning Star*

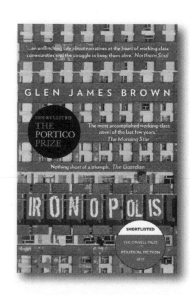

PARTHIAN Fiction

Martha, Jack & Shanco
CARYL LEWIS
TRANSLATED BY GWEN DAVIES
ISBN 978-1-912681-77-8
£9.99 • Paperback

Winner of the Wales Book of the Year
'Harsh, lyrical, devastating... sings with a
bitter poetry.' – *The Independent*

Love and Other Possibilities
LEWIS DAVIES
ISBN 978-1-906998-08-0
£6.99 • Paperback

Winner of the Rhys Davies Award
'Davies's prose is simple and effortless, the
kind of writing that wins competitions.'
– *The Independent*

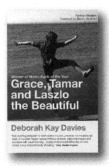

Grace, Tamar and Laszlo the Beautiful
DEBORAH KAY DAVIES
ISBN 978-1-912109-43-2
£8.99 • Paperback

Winner of the Wales Book of the Year
'Davies's writing thrills on all levels.'
– Suzy Ceulan Hughes

Hummingbird
TRISTAN HUGHES
ISBN 978-1-91090-90-8
£10 • Hardback
£8.99 • Paperback

Winner of the Stanford Fiction Award
'Superbly accomplished... Hughes's prose is
startling and luminous.' – *Financial Times*

PARTHIAN   Fiction

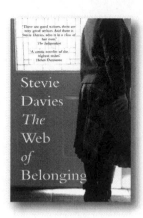

The Web of Belonging
STEVIE DAVIES
ISBN 978-1-912681-16-7
£8.99 • Paperback

'A comic novelist of
the highest order.'
– *The Times*

The Cormorant
STEPHEN GREGORY
ISBN 978-1-912681-69-3
£8.99 • Paperback
Winner of the
Somerset Maugham Award
'A first-class terror story with a
relentless focus that would have made
Edgar Allan Poe proud.'
– *The New York Times*

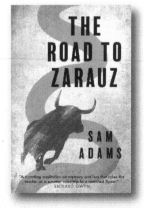

The Road to Zarauz
SAM ADAMS
ISBN 978-1-912681-85-3
£8.99 • Paperback
'A haunting meditation on memory and
loss that takes the reader on a summer
road trip to a vanished Spain.'
– Richard Gwyn

KISS AND TELL

Selected Stories

Foreword by **David Llewellyn**

JOHN SAM JONES

Parthian/**Modern**